Frantz Fanon for the 21st Century Volume 3

The Algerian Revolution, Islamic Discourse, the Colonizer and the Discourse of White Supremacy

Daurius Figueira

Table of Contents

Introduction

This is a deconstruction of Frantz Fanon's work first published in French in 1959 as "L' An Cinq, de la Revolution Algerienne" and in English in 1965 as "Studies in a Dying Colonialism" and thereafter as "A Dying Colonialism." As well as selected articles of Fanon on the Algerian Revolution published in the period 1957 to 1958 in the publication El Moudjahid of the FLN, collected and published in 1964 in French as "Pour la revolution Africaine" and in 1967 in English as "Toward the African Revolution." This deconstruction focuses on Fanon's discourse of Revolution as an abstract towards unearthing its discursive constructs, thereby laying bare Fanon's discourse of Revolution and specifically its application to the anti-colonial war of the Algerian masses against French colonial domination. This deconstruction reveals that Fanon's discourse of Revolution was one in which concepts that were anathema to each other were forced together to create an instrument of analysis of Revolution in a colonial context. Fanon's discourse, as Fanon's ideational output was in transition, searching for ideas that reflected our reality and served our liberation whilst culling white ideas, reformulating others and blending them with his own liberationary ideas in his thought process. Fanon's new liberationary ideational structure was a work in progress when his death in December 1961 ended this process out of which a new Fanon was emerging. This deconstruction interrogates Fanon's discourse of the Algerian Revolution, seeking insights into the failure of Fanon's model to explain the domination of the masses by a revolutionary oligarchy and the utilization of instruments of power to protect the hegemony of this revolutionary oligarchy, commonly used by the white colonizer under colonial domination in Algeria, since the Revolution. The course adopted by the Algerian Revolution since the defeat of the white colonizer was one not in keeping with Fanon's discourse of the Algerian Revolution. This is then a search for answers from Fanon, even though he died before liberation was attained in 1962. The Algerian Revolution has been jacked, the masses rendered powerless and in the 21st century Revolutionary Algeria is now immersed in/with the neo-colonial condition. Fanon never once in his writings admitted to this outcome, hence the quest of this work to understand why.

This is the final volume of the series "Frantz Fanon for the 21st century", the necessity of which was sparked by the developments in North Atlantic neo-liberal financial markets capitalism which went into meltdown in 2008. The mechanism unleashed by central banks of the North Atlantic to print trillions of units of their fiat currencies, especially the US dollar, has irretrievably changed the nature of the social orders of the North Atlantic and its political order. Quantitative Easing (QE) has changed the nature of the hegemonic oligarchies, deepened inequality and drives an assault on the mask of democracy, where instruments of power formulated under enslavement and colonial domination are now unleashed on the social orders of the metropoles.

These instruments of power are defined and contextualized by a 21st century discourse of white supremacy, which now identifies internal and external enemies as grave threats worthy of repression and elimination by any means necessary. The potent external threat envisaged is China, whilst all internal dissent is a threat that is contextualized in the manner massa did on the plantation and the colonizer did in the colonial state. The premier enemy is an enemy/non-white race, both internally and externally, hence the relevance of the oeuvre of Frantz Fanon in the 21st century. This is not then a resort to fascism as a result of a crisis of capitalism; which is itself another failed analytical product of a failed paradigm, i.e. – Leninist dialectical/historical materialism; but in actuality a return to a core discursive construct in the formation of the discourse of white supremacy in the eighteenth century. This is not neo-feudalism in the 21st century, but a return to the white supremacist discourse of non-white enslavement and colonial domination in the 21st century.

In this work I repeatedly use the concept "traditional Islam", which describes Islam in Algeria before colonial domination and its evolution under colonial domination. Islam in Algeria was incapable of resistance to the French colonial onslaught, as it was in itself engaged in an internal internecine war between Quranic discourse and those discourses intent on silencing Quranic discourse under a veneer of Islamic orthodoxy. This orthodoxy and its power relations failed to mount the resistance to French colonial domination demanded by Quranic discourse, seeking instead to retain its hegemony over Quranic discourse by forming a working accord with the colonizer. The colonizer, then through colonial domination, froze the evolution of the power relation between Quranic discourse and discourses intent on silencing Quranic discourse in favour of these usurper discourses. Under colonial domination, traditional Islam in Algeria intensified its separation and conflict with Quranic discourse, thereby destroying all intentions to recognize and mount an anti-colonial war of liberation. Traditional Islam in Algeria then became ossified, a fossil kept alive by the Muslim need to resist colonizer domination or the domination of Muslims by the kaffirun. In this fossilized condition Quranic discourse flowered and set about challenging both traditional Islam and the colonizer. The Revolutionary elite intervened into this power struggle with its use of the discourse Jihad to mobilize and motivate the Muslim masses to embrace the Revolution by embracing traditional Islam. The war for liberation from the colonizer in Algeria then enabled a new phase of the war for hegemony within Islam in Algeria as two streams emerged. One stream, traditional Islam, will embrace the discourse of Jihad through its various stages of evolution, where today it's expressed as Salafi-Jihadi Sunni discourse. The other will embrace the path of forming an Islamic alternate discourse to the discourse of the Revolutionary oligarchy, utilizing the institutions of the revolutionary state to challenge the oligarchy's hegemony. The concept of Jihad as a special, unique war only waged by Muslims as an absolute of traditional Islam and Salafi-Jihadi discourse is not Quranic. Jihad as an absolute is the product of white colonial domination of the Muslim lands, where Muslims burdened with hallucinatory whiteness embraced the discourse of the white Enlightenment in a supposed attempt to end colonial domination. The by-product of this process was Islamic Extremism, the gift white colonial domination acting in concert with its human product, non-whites afflicted with hallucinatory whiteness, gave to the world.

Chapter 1
"Preface July 1959"

In the preface Fanon states: "The Algerian war-the most hallucinatory war that any people has ever waged to smash colonial aggression. Its adversaries like to claim that the men who lead the Algerian Revolution are impelled by a thirst for blood. The democrats who were sympathetic to it repeat, for their part, that it has made mistakes." (Fanon 1965 pg. 23). The Algerian war of liberation is hallucinatory as the French refuse to recognizes the right to self-determination of the Algerian non-white peoples, nor their right to wage war for their liberation from French colonial domination. The strategy is then to demonize the Algerian as a blood crazed sub-human in need of French domination and civilization to curb this sub-human propensity. French colonial domination is then predicated on the discourse of white supremacy, which insists that in the 1950's French colonial white supremacist domination of Algeria is desirable, necessary and possible. This constitutes the French hallucinatory war of re-conquest, but its colonial nature does not separate it from all wars of re-conquest waged by the North Atlantic since the Algerian war, especially by the USA, for they are all hallucinatory in nature. From Vietnam to the War on Terror, they are driven by the white supremacist discourse and its worldview that demands white hegemony over the non-white races of the world. Fanon indicates that in France the opposition to Algerian resistance to French hegemony embraces the range of political discourses and worldviews for they are all rooted in the discourse of white supremacy. Fanon now speaks to the hallucinatory war of the Algerians: "It has in fact happened that Algerian citizens have violated the directives of the commanding bodies, and that things that should have been avoided have transpired on the national soil. Almost always, these concerned Algerian citizens." (Fanon 1965 pg. 23). Fanon is here apologetic for the spontaneous acts of violence that always flow with resistance to colonial domination, that predominantly involve non-white on non-white violence. Spontaneous violence is a product of the psycho-existential complex, yet a necessary stage in the process to destroy the psycho-existential complex. Spontaneous violence must be allowed to flower and then disciplined by a wider national strategy of revolution. The top down approach of the Algerian Revolution, that Fanon was here advocating, destroyed the mass control of the revolution which became glaringly evident with the civil war of the 1990's. In his final book, The Wretched of the Earth, Fanon was in fact revealing the future of the Algerian Revolution. The apologetic extends to the identity of the victims of spontaneous violence namely non-white, French colonizers. Fanon continues in this vein: "In a war of liberation, the colonized people must win, but they must do so without 'barbarity.' The European nation that practices torture is a blighted nation, unfaithful to its history. The underdeveloped nation that practices torture thereby confirms its nature, plays the role of an underdeveloped people. If it does not wish to be morally condemned by the 'Western nations,' an underdeveloped nation is obliged to practice fair play, even while the adversary ventures, with a clear conscience, into the unlimited exploration of new means of terror." (Fanon 1965 pg. 24). The salient, overriding reality is not the war of liberation against French colonial domination, but a war of liberation being waged against white colonial domination under the hegemony of a world order under the hegemony of a discourse of white supremacy; with this hegemonic white supremacist discourse willing and able to use its power to subvert and co-opt the Algerian revolution as its vassal, which it successfully did. The focus on, even the fixation of, evicting French colonial domination of Algeria without due regard for the much more potent onslaught which followed the victory of the revolution enabled the rolling over of the revolution. To withstand the onslaught of the neo-colonial instrument of power unleashed with victory over French colonial domination, the very nature of power relations between the masses and the leadership must be drastically different from what they were during the war of liberation from colonial domination. Fanon continues as follows: "Because we want a democratic and a renovated Algeria, because we believe one cannot rise and liberate oneself in one area and sink in another, we condemn, with pain in our hearts, those brothers who have flung themselves into revolutionary action with the almost physiological brutality that centuries of oppression give rise to and feed." (Fanon 1965 pg. 25). The war of liberation does not then embrace the release of centuries of white oppression, barbarity and torture seeking catharsis through physiological brutality. The war of liberation is fought in keeping with international law with rules of war formulated by hegemonic whites, who themselves never abide by it, yet insist we abide by it when we do battle with them. The war of liberation must then offer no instrument of power to destroy the colonial psycho-existential complex nor establish counter measures in the psyche of the liberated Algerian to resist the assault of the neo-colonial psycho-existential complex. The masses unleash spontaneous acts of violence in response to the shifting of the power relations and the need to self-medicate to end the gnawing hollow that colonial domination bores in our psyche. This is not acceptable revolutionary behavior as defined by leadership debilitated with the colonial psycho-existential complex embracing a Leninist concept of revolution seeped in its white hegemonic worldview. How does this revolutionary leadership plagued with hallucinatory whiteness purge itself of the colonial psycho-existential complex and resist the neo-colonial psycho-existential complex? It does not, that is why in the 20th and 21st centuries the Algerian revolution has failed the Algerian masses. And Fanon falsified this work with his final work. Fanon's apologetic continues: "It is not easy to conduct, with a minimum of errors, the struggles of a people, sorely tried by a hundred and thirty years of domination, against an enemy as determined and as ferocious as French colonialism." (Fanon 1965 pg. 26). The colonized Algerian is the victim of French colonial domination of specific pedigree which exonerates the Algerian revolution of the mistakes it has made in the course of the revolution. There is then a hierarchy of colonial domination with French Algerian colonialism at the apex thereby exonerating the Algerian revolution of its few mistakes made. Fanon is fixating on this revolution, thereby betraying his white worldview yet to be purged, the product of the colonial psycho-existential complex. In this white worldview, the experience of white colonial hegemony is then different in Algeria from that of Martinique, thereby creating objective and subjective conditions for revolution which do not exist in Martinique. Algeria, and its revolutionary potential, is then superior to that of Martinique measured against the yardstick of revolution against colonial domination. Algeria and its revolution then becomes Fanon's fetish, constituted by his embrace of a Leninist worldview with all the pitfalls in its theory of historical and dialectical materialism wrapped up in a discourse of white supremacy. In this work, Fanon labors under the yoke of this Leninist worldview applied to a colonial reality. Fanon continues with his discourse of the uniqueness of the Algerian revolution: "No one thought that France would defend foot by foot this shameless colonialism for five years, a colonialism which is matched, on the continent, by its homologue in South Africa. Nor did anyone suspect that the Algerian people would make its place in history with such intensity." (Fanon 1965 pg. 26). Why would anyone knowledgeable of French politics and the current actions undertaken by white colonialists to protect their white settlers, especially the British as in Kenya, not expect the French to hold on to Algeria by any means necessary? Fanon is insisting on the uniqueness of French colonial aggression in Algeria in an attempt to exalt and proclaim the revolutionary specificity and uniqueness of the Algerian revolution. But in his third and final book, Fanon presented the instruments of an analysis which, when applied to Algeria indicated that the failure of the revolution to liberate the masses was inevitable, which became palpable in the civil war of the 1990's. The discourse of the exaltation of the Algerian revolution continues as follows: "There is in Algeria, as the Algerian people see it, an irreversible situation. French colonialism itself has recognized it, and it attempts, anarchically, to tag along behind the historic movement." "One has a duty to understand this entrenchment in a war which has all the earmarks of a morbid infatuation. We want to show in this first study that on the Algerian soil a new society has come to birth. The men and women of Algeria today resemble neither those of 1930 nor those of 1954, nor yet those of 1957. The old Algeria is dead. All the innocents blood that has flowed onto the national soil has produced a new humanity and no one must fail to recognize this fact." (Fanon 1965 pgs. 27-28). The Revolution has created a new Algerian, whilst destroying the old colonial order, but is this process of renewal sustainable across time is the crux of the matter, for by the civil war of the 1990's it is now clear that a neo-colonial Algeria has emerged in need of a revolution of national liberation. A revolution that destroys colonial control does not immunize the new nation created from servility to neo-colonial domination and its assault on the masses. Great exaltation and the fetishisation of the new nation enables neo-colonial domination premised on the hegemony of a post-colonial oligarchy, rooted in division of the masses through racism, as elucidated by Fanon in his final work. Fanon continues: "While in many colonial countries it is the independence acquired by a party that progressively informs the diffused national consciousness of the people, in Algeria it is the national consciousness, the collective suffering and terrors that make it inevitable that the people take its destiny into its own hands." (Fanon 1965 pg. 28). This Algerian national consciousness that drives the masses failed miserably in the post-colonial Algeria to pre-empt the creation of a national oligarchy and the hegemony it wields to the detriment of the interests of the said masses. This national consciousness failed miserably to resist the instruments of power unleashed by the oligarchs that divided the masses on the basis of race, ethnicity, tribe and clan and in the 1990's to prevent the slide to civil war for the preservation of the hegemony of this oligarchy. In the post-colonial nation, this much vaunted revolutionary national consciousness is then open to assault and manipulation by instruments of power constituted under colonial domination, now utilized by the Algerian oligarchy. This reality then indicates that the much vaunted national revolutionary consciousness was not purged of the colonial psycho-existential complex which was evolved into the neo-colonial complex and unleashed on the masses by the Algerian oligarchy. This served the conjuncture of their interests and that of the white supremacist North Atlantic. The Algerian revolution is then a potent symbol of the schizophrenia of the colonized Third World where a revolution surrendered to an Algerian oligarchy serving their interests and that of the North Atlantic, to the detriment of the masses of Algeria. So much for the mythic, Leninist concept of the revolution as an absolute totality. Fanon continues: "We want to show in these pages that *colonialism has definitely lost out in Algeria, whilst the Algerians, come what may, have definitely won*." "An army can at any time reconquer the ground lost, but how can the inferiority complex, the fear and despair of the past be re-implanted in the consciousness of the peoples?" "The power of the Algerian Revolution henceforth resides in the radical mutation that the Algerian has undergone." (Fanon 1965 pg. 31-32). The victory of the Algerian Revolution over French white supremacist colonial domination and the grave price that will be paid for re-conquest of Algeria is a given. But with victory there is a much more potent threat which Fanon cannot see, the threat that emanates from the revolution itself, on the issue of the nature of the power relations that arise and the construction of hegemony in the new social order. Ultimately, the concentration of power in the hands of a small national oligarchy emerged to the detriment of the masses and the revolution.

The Revolution, Colonial Domination and the Khimar

In chapter one of the text Fanon deals with the Khimar/veil, French colonial domination, the Algerian woman and the Revolution. Fanon states: "The way people clothe themselves, together with the traditions of dress and finery that custom implies, constitutes the most distinctive form of a society's uniqueness, that is to say the one that is the most immediately perceptible." "The fact of belonging to a given cultural group is usually revealed by a clothing tradition." "but the veil worn by the women with such constancy that it generally suffices to characterize Arab society." (Fanon 1965 pg. 35). The Muslims under the domination of French white supremacist colonialism now indicate their cultural uniqueness, their difference from that of the colonial overlord through the wearing of the khimar/veil by female Muslims. The khimar denotes difference, separation and much more to the French overlord as it illustrates Muslim intransigence in the face of the concerted colonial attack on Islam to constitute a Muslim plagued with hallucinatory whiteness, the very basis of being a munafique. The strategic importance of the khimar for Fanon is as follows: "With the veil, things become well-defined and ordered. The Algerian woman in the eyes of the observer is unmistakably 'she who hides behind a veil.'" (Fanon 1965 pg. 36). The khimar is then utilized as a symbol of resistance and protest with the adoption of the black khimar, which is using the white man's symbolism to send a message to the white colonial overlord. Fanon states: "It is worth noting that black, in Moroccan or Arab society, has never expressed mourning or affliction. As a combat measure, the adoption of black is a response to the desire to exert a symbolic pressure on the occupier, and hence to make a logical choice of one's own symbols." (Fanon 1965 pg. 36). The khimar is much more than an instrument of resistance and defiance to colonial domination. It is most of all, an attempt to hide the body of the Muslim woman from the gaze of the male colonial overlord, as he demands his right and entitlement to sexual harvesting of the colonized. A discourse of the hijab was formulated to contest the French colonial entitlement to sexually harvest the colonized, specifically the entitlement operationalised by white colonizers over Muslim females. French colonialism in Algeria by necessity engaged in a war for hegemony with the discourse of the hijab. Fanon continues: "We shall see that this veil, one of the elements of the traditional Algerian garb, was to become the bone of contention in a grandiose battle, on which the occupation force were to mobilize their most powerful and most varied resources, and in the course of which the colonized were to display a surprising force of inertia." (Fanon 1965 pgs. 36-37). The discourse of the hijab as a weapon against white colonial domination constituted the white colonial assault which continues to this day. As is the case with white supremacist imperialism, it distorts the power relations of non-white peoples on crucial issues, effectively redefining and hobbling all efforts at change, arising from power relations free from the distortions arising from white colonial imperialist interference. The colonial assault was intent on destroying the hegemony of the discourse of the hijab, thereby emancipating Muslim women to adopt white values and make themselves available for white sexual harvesting. This was the weapon to assault the resistance of the Muslim male. Fanon states: "The officials of the French administration in Algeria, committed to destroying the people's originality, and under instruction to bring about the disintegration, at whatever cost, of forms of reality likely to evoke a national reality directly or indirectly, were to concentrate their efforts on the wearing of the veil, which was looked upon at this juncture as a symbol of the status of the Algerian woman. Such a position is not the consequence of a chance intuition." (Fanon 1965 pg. 37). The khimar, the discourse of the hijab that constitutes it, is assaulted by the colonial overlord as the key to erasing any Muslim resistance rooted in a national identity, of a free, decolonized Algeria. This is a multifaceted assault to sexualise the Muslim woman for the benefit of the white, male colonizer. To strip the hijab away and reveal the body hidden away from the gaze of the white male colonizer, thereby attaching desire to this revealed body, attaching the soul constituted by white desire that sexualises the Muslim female. The sexualisation of the Muslim female then dismantles the basis of the Muslim social order and its sexual politics towards destroying the Revolution. Fanon insists that this was a planned assault informed by the white, scientific discourses of French academia. White, French academia produced the specific discourse of the Muslim woman and her place in the social order that was the key to breaking the back of the Revolution. Fanon describes this white discourse as follows: "Beneath the patrilineal pattern of Algerian society, the specialists described a structure of matrilineal essence. Arab society has often been presented by Westerners as a formal society in which outside appearances

12

are paramount. The Algerian woman, an intermediary between obscure forces and the group, appeared in this perspective to assume a primordial importance. Behind the visible, manifest patriarchy, the more significant existence of a basic matriarchy was affirmed." (Fanon 1965 pg. 37). The white, racist, academic, scientific discourse insisted that beneath the public face of patriarchy there existed a matriarchy that was the base of the social order in which patriarchy was rooted. The key to destroying the Revolution then, was to target the Muslim women with a specific discourse formulated for the purpose of destroying the matriarchal foundation of the patriarchy. To do this it is necessary to convince Muslim women that they are oppressed by the Muslim male and the patriarchy and the symbol of this oppression is the khimar driven by the discourse of the hijab. Destroy the hegemony of the discourse of the hijab and sexualise the Muslim woman setting her on her path to hallucinatory whiteness, thereby attaining the conquest of the Muslim male. Fanon continues: "This enabled the colonial administration to define a precise political doctrine. 'If we want to destroy the structure of Algerian society, its capacity for resistance, we must first of all conquer the woman; we must first of all go and find them behind the veil where they hide themselves and in the houses where the men keep them out of sight.'" (Fanon 1965 pgs. 37-38). A white feminist discourse is formulated and unleashed in the 1950's in Algeria, informed by a concept of the sexual politics of the Algerian social order, that enables and justifies an instrument of power to destroy the Revolution, towards maintenance of white, French, colonial, imperial domination of non-white

peoples. This white feminist discourse still has traction in the 21st century as the War on Terror has breathed new life into it. Fanon continues: "It is the position of women that was accordingly taken as the theme of action. The dominant administration solemnly undertook to defend this woman, pictured as humiliated, sequestered, cloistered...It described immense possibilities of women, unfortunately transformed by the Algerian man into an inert, demonetized, indeed dehumanized object. The behavior of the Algerian was very firmly denounced and described as medieval and barbaric." "Around the family life of the Algerian, the occupier piled up a whole mass of judgments, appraisals, reasons, accumulated anecdotes and edifying examples, thus attempting to confine the Algerian with a circle of guilt." (Fanon 1965 pg. 38).

A white feminist, colonial, imperial discourse was now assaulting the psyche of the Algerian intent on convincing the Algerian female that the the Algerian male was barbaric, an oppressor of the Algerian female. The strategic intent was to problematise the Algerian family, through embracing and internalizing the guilt of being inferior non-white beings in need of French civilization. The Revolution was then an Algerian male construct, designed to ensure the Algerian woman remain trapped in barbarism and a medieval social order, hence endemic backwardness. Hallucinatory whiteness was then the only viable path to modernity and progress. The core concepts of this discourse are in no way unique as they flow from the white supremacist Christian discourse of African enslavement in the West Indies. Fanon continues: "After it had been posited that the woman constituted the pivot of Algerian society, all efforts were made to obtain control over her." "In the colonialist program, it was the woman, who was given the historic mission of shaking up the Algerian man. Converting the woman, winning her over to the foreign values, wrenching her free from her status, was at the same time achieving a real power over the man and attaining a practical, effective means of destructuring Algerian culture." "Still today, in 1959, the dream of a total domestication of Algerian society by means of 'unveiled women aiding and sheltering the occupier' continues to haunt the colonial authorities." (Fanon 1965 pgs. 38-39). The discourse of the white colonial overlord insists that the key to victory over the Revolution is the unveiled Algerian woman, the unveiled Muslim woman. A non-white woman fully exposed to the gaze of the white overlord, sexualised and available for sexual harvesting is the only means, the instrument of power to defeat the Revolution by collapsing the social order of the colonized non-whites. The unveiling of the Muslim woman illustrates in public spaces that the non-white woman is finally available and receptive to white power, expressed through sexual harvesting by white males. The use of rape as an instrument of war by French colonial forces potently illustrated this desire. There is also an assault on the Algerian male in the employ of the white occupier to present his wife to the gaze of the white society and to publicly adopt what is considered the acceptable white lifestyle. Contact with the white occupier then opens one to pressure to abide by white values exhibited by a servile, obedient non-white employee. Fanon states: "would bring out the sadistic and perverse character of these contacts and relationships and would show in microcosm the tragedy

14

of the colonial situation on the psychological level, the way the two systems directly confront each other, the epic of the colonized society, with its specific ways of existing, in the face of the colonialist hydra." (Fanon 1965 pg. 40). In its quest to defeat the Revolution and ensure its hegemony over Algeria, the white supremacist colonizer has then declared war on Islamic discourse. The Revolution is seen as being rooted in and springing from the alternate discourse and worldview that is Islamic discourse. The white supremacist colonizer views this engagement as a war against Islamic discourse for the soul of the Algerian and it is the imperative that the soul of the Algerian woman be first conquered. The Algerian, Muslim woman is then the weak link in the chain, the bond with Islamic discourse. A white supremacist, feminist colonial discourse that is rooted in white patriarchy is formulated and unleashed in Algeria. Then reformulated for the women of the Iranian Islamic Revolution, then Afghanistan, Pakistan, Iraq, Somalia etc. as it serves white supremacist hegemony, whilst articulated by non-white women as an agent of liberation from patriarchy. Such is the tragedy of hallucinatory whiteness in a neo-colonial context. White supremacist hegemony demands a relentless assault on our culture and worldview that enables us through an alternate worldview to resist, for resistance springs from this alternate view. Fanon states: "The method of presenting the Algerian as a prey fought over with equal ferocity by Islam and France with its Western culture reveals the whole approach of the occupier, his philosophy and his policy." "What is in fact the assertion of a distinct identity, concern with keeping intact a few shreds of national existence, is attributed to religion, magical, fanatical behavior." (Fanon 1965 pg. 41). The white colonizer problematises the resistance of the Algerian, to the domination of their indigenous culture by white colonial culture, by defining this quest to ensure the survival of their non-colonial identity, as the product of barbaric backwardness fostered by Islamic discourse, with its non-rational basis rooted in magic and its warrior ethic based fanaticism. The white colonizer then speaks of the Revolution as a last gasp against acculturation by an inherently superior white, French culture. The Revolution is then a retrograde step in an attempt to hold on to Islamic backwardness and barbarity rejecting white modernity and progress. The drive for hegemony by the white supremacist North Atlantic, can only be expressed via their penchant for the Manichean duality, which drives their extremist worldview. Fanon states: "More precisely, the phenomenon of counter acculturation must be understood as the organic impossibility of a culture to modify any one of its customs without at the same time re-evaluating its deepest values, its most stable models. To speak of counter-acculturation in a colonial situation is an absurdity. The phenomenon of resistance observed in the colonized must be related to an attitude of counter-assimilation, of maintenance of a cultural, hence national, originality." (Fanon 1965 pg. 42). The Revolution is not an instance of counter-acculturation, as it is used to mask the reality of white colonial domination, where a national non-white culture, worldview and the discourses that drive them are under assault to be immersed and silenced, by an imposed foreign, alien, white supremacist discourse with its worldview and culture attached. This has nothing to do with acculturation but with assimilation by conquest. Fanon is painstakingly presenting the evidence that in its quest for hegemony all truth is manufactured by the white supremacist North Atlantic to serve its strategic interests. Truth is a weapon, an instrument of power constituted to serve white supremacist hegemony, which illustrates that the quest is predicated on hegemony at the level of the idea. We are then colonized and gleefully embrace neo-colonial domination as we are subservient at the level of the idea.

The abandonment of the khimar by Muslim women then sent signals to the white colonizer, signals of success, of victory, of docility and servitude. Fanon states: "Every new Algerian woman unveiled announced to the occupier an Algerian society whose systems of defense were in the process of dislocation, open and breached. Every veil that fell, every body that became liberated from the traditional embrace of the haik, every face that offered itself to the bold and impatient glance of the occupier, was a negative expression of the fact that Algeria was beginning to deny herself and was accepting the rape of the colonizer." (Fanon 1965 pg. 42). The white colonizer interprets the unveiling as surrender and acceptance of domination, including sexual harvesting by the white colonizer, as rape is both graphically literal and figurative. Fanon now presents his position that the white colonizer expresses desire for the Muslim woman that demands her unveiling, the desire of the white dominant colonizer claiming his right, entitlement to sexually harvest the colonized woman. Fanon states: "A strand of hair, a bit of forehead, a segment of an 'overwhelmingly beautiful' face glimpsed in a streetcar or on a train, may suffice to keep alive and strengthen the European's persistence in his irrational conviction that the Algerian woman is the queen of all women. But there is also in the European the crystallization of an aggressiveness, the strain of a kind of violence before the Algerian woman. Unveiling this woman is revealing her beauty, it is baring her secret, breaking her resistance, making her available for adventure." "There is in it the will to bring the woman within its reach, to make her a possible object of possession. This woman who sees without being seen frustrates the colonizer." (Fanon 1965 pgs. 43-44). The Muslim woman is an object of white colonizer desire necessary to expressing white supremacist hegemony over the Algerians. Domination must be expressed via its instrument of sexual harvesting and the willingness of the colonized to be sexually harvested, to be perpetually ready and available for white sexual harvesting. The khimar then expresses the resistance of the Muslim woman to white domination and their unavailability to be sexually harvested. Domination must be expressed by desire and the willingness to be dominated by whites, one such instrument is sexual harvesting and the availability for sexual harvesting. The khimar is defined by the white colonizer as the expression of resistance to domination as it signals that Muslim women are unavailable and resisting white sexual harvesting. This discourse insists that white domination is premised on the acceptance of specific sexual relations and sexual values, which enable white sexual harvesting, which are anathema to Islamic sexual values and codes of permitted/halal and prohibited/haraam human action. This discourse is then demanding the dismantling of the Islamic code of sexual values, replacing it with pragmatic nihilism as the guidepost to sexual behavior, thereby enabling and facilitating white domination.

There is a psychology of the colonizer with reference to the veiled Muslim non-white woman which ultimately embraces violent possession and exploitation. Fanon states: "At the level of the psychological strata of the occupier, the evocation of this freedom given to the sadism of the conqueror, to his eroticism, creates faults, fertile gaps through which both dreamlike forms of behavior and, criminal acts can emerge." (Fanon 1965 pg. 45). The right/ entitlement of white sexual harvesting embraces violence, sadism, possession, the taking and collection of trophies and serial murder. There is a dream state to this physical reality where the worldview of sexual harvesting of non-whites are played out, expressed and rehearsed to its extremes. Fanon states: "With an Algerian woman, there is no progressive conquest, no mutual revelation. Straight off, with the maximum of violence, there is possession, rape, near-murder. The act assumes a para-neurotic brutality and sadism even in a normal European. This brutality and this sadism are in fact emphasized by the frightened attitude of the Algerian woman." (Fanon 1965 pg. 46). In their dream state, the white colonizer segregated his dreams as the Muslim woman was the weak, fawning object that he sexualised, raped and destroyed whilst dreams of white women were those befitting the female of the master race. Fanon has now placed his hands on the reality that white supremacist hegemony must involve sexual harvesting of non-white women and the wrapping of their bodies in a soul that sexualises them and constitutes a moral order, through which they view the world that enables white supremacist sexual harvesting and domination. This applies to both sexes.

Fanon now speaks to the dynamic of resistance involving the resistance to the assault on the veil by Algerians, in that it is a response to an assault of the colonizer on the terrain of engagement as defined by the colonizer. This is then the inherent flaw of such resistance, where the colonized are seduced to resist an assault on the terrain of the colonizer, utilizing the ideas of the colonizer. As in the case of Algeria you can very well win the war against colonial domination but surrender amicably to neo-colonial domination. By responding to the assault on the veil by embracing the veil you are engaging with the white supremacists on their terms; for this is reaction, not revolutionary preemptive action. By embracing the veil as resistance you are confirming the white discourse of the veil and affirming its potency. Fanon states: "It was the colonialist's frenzy to unveil the Algerian woman, it was his gamble on his winning the battle of the veil at whatever cost, that were to provoke the native's bristling resistance" "We here recognize one of the laws of the psychology of colonization. In an initial phase, it is the action, the plans of the occupier that determines the centers of resistance around which a people's will to survive becomes organized." (Fanon 1965 pgs. 46-47). The colonizer's aggression against specific expressions of national identity, constitutes the resistance of the colonized; which enables the colonizer long after colonization

18

has formally ended to continue the assault under the neo-colonial condition. Resistance/ rebellion against colonial domination does not constitute liberation, especially at the level of the idea; for liberation is only constituted when revolution is informed by a discourse that is an alternate, alien and in contradiction to white supremacist North Atlantic discourse. This is the lesson of Fanon's final work, not this work presently being deconstructed. The Algerian Revolution ended French colonial domination, but was defeated by neo-colonial domination, as a result of its failure to formulate and unleash this alternate discourse rooted in a new, post-colonial vision of Islam. Fanon continues on his concept of revolution being absolute as follows: "It is the white man who creates the Negro, But it is the Negro who creates negritude. To the colonial offensive against the veil, the colonized opposes the cult of the veil. What was an undifferentiated element in a homogeneous whole acquires a taboo character, and the attitude of the given Algerian woman with respect to the veil will be constantly related to her overall attitude with respect to the foreign domination." (Fanon 1965 pg. 47). The colonized opposes the white colonizer's fixation with the veil with their own fixation on the veil, which becomes part of a defensive position, which enables the embrace of the Salafi-Jihadi worldview and its eventual challenge to the hegemony of the revolutionary oligarchy that unleashed the civil war of the 1990's. The negro is the soul created by the white supremacist to enclose the body of the African and negritude is the product of that soul of the negro. Reveling in being a negro is then celebrating the hegemony of white supremacy and affirming the inferiority of the negro, as the inherent superiority of the white is proclaimed. Liberation is not possible via utilizing the discourse of negritude, negritude is simply shucking and jiving in praise of massa. The assault of the white colonialist on the veil then unleashed a response which was not informed by a liberationary discourse rooted in a new, revolutionary vision of Islam, which potently illustrated the reality of the absence of a liberationary discourse driving the Algerian revolution. Fanon states: "The tenacity of the occupier in his endeavor to unveil the women, to make of them an ally in the work of cultural destruction, has the effect of strengthening the traditional patterns of behavior. These patterns, which were essentially positive in the strategy of resistance to the corrosive action of the colonizer, naturally had negative effects." (Fanon 1965 pg. 49). The assault of the white colonizer on the khimar breathed new life into the traditional form of Islam, which failed miserably to resist the white colonial incursion and eventually to constitute a revolutionary war for its destruction. The white colonizer's discourse of the veil caught the leadership of the revolutionary movement totally unprepared to answer this threat potently from its secular, Leninist discourse of the revolution as absolute. The colonizer's discourse of the veil reawakened traditional Islam from its slumber by framing the defense of the veil within the framework of traditional Islamic totalist discourse, which prepared the terrain for the assault on the revolutionary state by Islamic Extremism as it faltered under the hegemony of the revolutionary oligarchy.

The reluctance of the revolutionary elite to include Muslim women as combatants against the colonizer reveals the inherent ambivalence of a secular, Leninist discourse in a social order dominated by an Islamic worldview. The revolutionary leadership was in itself on a path of deception of the masses, hence their refusal to formulate and unleash a revolutionary Islamic discourse as the driver of the anti-colonial revolution, as they saw no room for this discourse in their revolution. The revolutionary leadership questioned the fitness of the Muslim woman for revolutionary war given her daily life as a Muslim woman. Fanon states: "This relatively cloistered life, with its known, categorized, regulated comings and goings, made any immediate revolution seem a dubious proposition." "To this doubt there was added an equally important element. The leaders hesitated to involve the women, being perfectly aware of the ferocity of the colonizer." (Fanon 1965 pg. 49). The leaders of the revolution viewed the traditional Islamic discourse as a hindrance to revolution and a threat as it provided spaces in the social order open for exploitation by the white colonizer. This leadership welcomed the white colonial assault on the khimar as it opened up the traditional Islamic order to assault creating space for the secular, Leninist discourse to seek and exert hegemony over the social order. But their choice of discourse breeds the resistance to the revolution that is proving to be much more resilient than white colonization; i.e. – the resistance of Islamic Extremism.

The need to respond to the total anti-revolutionary war unleashed by the white colonizer forced the hand of the revolutionary leadership to now include

Muslim women in the anti-colonial war. For Fanon this was an entry into war for Muslim women that was unprecedented hence devoid of precedent, practice and history. Fanon states: 'It is an authentic birth in a pure state, without preliminary instruction. There is no character to imitate. On the contrary, there is an intense dramatization, a continuity between the woman and the revolutionary. The Algerian woman rises directly to the level of tragedy." (Fanon 1965 pg. 50). The Muslim woman and the revolution are merged, welded together by the tragedy of resistance against the colonial overlord. But the central issue is the post-liberation reality and the women in a revolutionary social order. The power abrogated from the masses by the oligarchy specifically impacts women, especially in a social order where no discourse of revolutionary Islam has replaced traditional Islam on the ground, as the hegemonic discourse driving the social order. The revolutionary social order exhibits then the condition of multiple discourses contending for hegemony through armed conflict, brutal repression and thought control. Persons traversing the varied terrain of the social order must then be accomplished in communicating and acting according to multiple discourses exerting hegemony over specific spaces. One has to develop multiple personalities to be socialized.

The Muslim woman as an active agent of the revolution has to be de-veiled, adopt French cultural mannerisms, dress and fashion and display her body and sexuality to freely operate in the French settler urban centers. Fanon states: "The protective mantle of the Kasbah, the almost organic curtain of safety that the Arab town weaves around the native, withdrew, and the Algerian woman, exposed, was sent forth into the conqueror's city. Very quickly she adopted an absolutely unbelievable offensive tactic." "The European city is not the prolongation of the native city. The colonizers have not settled in the midst of the natives. They have surrounded the native city; they have laid siege to it. Every exit from the Kasbah of Algiers opens on enemy territory." "The native cities are deliberately caught in the conqueror's vice." Fanon 1965 pgs. 51-52). The awakening of the Muslim woman to revolutionary action is tragedy, as her commitment has no historical or cultural groundings as she walks willingly into the maelstrom of the settler city, making it up as she goes along. She is tragedy, for during her action for the revolution she faces the uncertainty of traversing the spaces under the hegemony of traditional Islam, whilst there is no revolutionary Islamic discourse forthcoming from the leaders of the revolution to affirm her action, all they offer is an alien white secular discourse of the revolution as absolute, insisting that she walk away from her traditional Islamic grounding. With victory the nascent oligarchy abrogates the power of the revolutionary masses unto themselves, choking the power of the masses, encapsulating them in a repressive state utilizing the divisions of race, ethnicity, geography, clan and tribe to render them pliant and subservient. In this revolutionary state, the oligarchy intensifies her tragedy, as opportunity is denied her and the alien secular discourse offers no solace, comfort nor progress, whilst the oligarchs grow filthy rich and opulent and wield the power of life and death over her. She returns to her Islamic groundings, but by now traditional Islam has been replaced with Salafi-Jihadi Sunni Islam and at the point in time the battle for hegemony is launched with the oligarchs the death of the Revolution is confirmed. The Revolution was the product of French colonial domination and in keeping with its origin in a hegemonic white discourse, with victory it quickly evolved into a neo-colonial dictatorship in the service of its hegemonic oligarchs and the white overlords. Fanon continues: "The Algerian woman, the young Algerian woman-must overcome a multiplicity of inner resistances, of subjectively organized fears, of emotions. She must at the same time confront the essentially hostile world of the occupier and the mobilized, vigilant, and efficient police forces. Each time she ventures into the European city, the Algerian woman must achieve a victory over herself, over her childish fears." "Initially subjective, the breaches made in colonialism are the result of a victory of the colonized over their old fear and over the atmosphere of despair distilled day after day by a colonialism that has incrusted itself with the *prospect of enduring forever.*" (Fanon 1965 pgs. 52-53). The requirements for defeating the colonial occupation is all encompassing, demanding the honing of a new personality and worldview specifically designed to defeat and oust the colonial occupier. But this new personality and worldview has very little utility and specific value to preparing the personality and worldview for revolutionary people's democracy and power and a new social order rooted in this new worldview. The anti-colonial worldview and personality aids and abets the formation and hegemony of the revolutionary oligarchy, the division and fragmentation of the masses into warring factions and the capture of the revolutionary state by the oligarchs, including the ruling elite of the revolutionary armed forces. What was deemed vitally necessary and required (the revolutionary vanguard/elite) to making a successful anti-colonial revolution in the context of Algeria, became the most powerful enemy of the Revolution after victory over the colonizer. The instrument to defeat the colonial occupier is in fact the locomotive of the neo-colonial condition Algeria is in since the anti-colonial revolution. This is so because the ideas of the colonizer were used to drive the Revolution to remove the colonizer, there was no Algerian revolution of the idea.

Fanon now compares the action of the Muslim woman who has removed her khimar and entered the European city as a revolutionary fighter as the Algerian males who have volunteered for a suicide attack on the occupier (fidai). Fanon states: "Every blow dealt the Revolution, every massacre perpetrated by the adversary, intensified the ferocity of the colonialists and hemmed in the Algerian civilian on all sides." "From this point on the Algerian woman became wholly and deliberately immersed in the revolutionary action." "During this period Algerians caught in the European city were pitilessly challenged, arrested and searched." (Fanon 1965 pgs 56-57). The Muslim woman unveiled was now placed in the gravest peril by being operationalized in the European cities. The only viable way to operate successfully in the European cities was then to strip away all that constituted and signaled to the gaze that she was a Muslim woman. The revolutionary Muslim woman was called upon to adopt the culture of the white, European woman in order to ensure a successful operation on her part. Whilst the fidai/shahid Algerian males were not called upon to make such strategic shifts in their culture as they chose death through attacks on the colonizer. Fanon states: "This is why we must watch the parallel progress of this man and this woman, of the couple that brings death to the enemy, life to the Revolution. The one radically transformed into a European woman, poised and unconstrained, whom no one will suspect, completely at home in the environment, and the other, a stranger, tense, moving toward his destiny." (Fanon 1965 pg. 57). The male shahid is alien to this world but he is there to die for the Revolution, enabled by the Muslim woman who has now immersed herself in the white soul that attaches to her body to constitute her an Arab plagued with hallucinatory whiteness, hence a fit and able Arab.

Whilst the male shahid accepts death rather than life for the Revolution but the motivation to do so is not revealed by Fanon. But this now fit and able Arab woman also faces death, torture, rape and imprisonment with every mission she undertakes into the colonizer's city, and is not deemed a shahid by the revolutionary leadership. Fanon now insists that the male fidai is not an anarchist nor a terrorist as the fidai is a specific reality generated by the Algerian Revolution. Fanon states: "The fidai, on the other hand, has a rendezvous with the life of the Revolution, and with his own life. The fidai is not one of the sacrificed. To be sure, he does not shrink from the possibility of losing his life, or the independence of the country, but at no moment does he choose death." (Fanon 1965 pgs. 57-58). Unlike the terrorist, the fidai is not chasing death, is desirous of death's embrace, but will not shrink from embracing death for the furtherance of the Revolution and the freedom of Algeria. The fidai has no need to embrace whiteness in order to accomplish his mission, unlike the Arab woman. The fidai is then the apex of the hierarchy of ideal personages of the Revolutionary idyllic of the Algerian discourse of the Revolution. But the unveiled Algerian woman entering the colonizer's city to make war on the colonizer never attains the condition of being Shahid, for she is unveiled. A discourse which uses the discourse of Jihad as the justification for its military action against the colonizer, as the legitimization for the military action and as the main motivational instrument for male Algerians to join the revolutionary force. The sensibilities of traditional Islam were adhered to, as clearly the revolutionary leaders believed that their secular, Leninist discourse would alienate them from a predominantly Islamic Algerian worldview. The discourse of the revolutionary leader manipulated Islamic discourse to mask their non-Islamic stance, which with freedom drove this revolutionary elite to quickly exert hegemony over the Muslim masses. In their strategy of embracing Islamic discourse to mask their non-Islamic credentials, they kept traditional Islam alive, thereby paving the way for the entry and spread of Salafi-Jihadi discourse and its eventual challenge to the hegemony of the revolutionary oligarchs. The strategy also ensured that there was always present in revolutionary Algeria an alternate discourse to that of Islam, masking secular Leninism yet alluding to Islamic credentials. By the decade of the 1990's the masses simply chose the Islamic alternative that the revolutionary elite gave space to and this elite responded with the expected repression and suppression leading to the civil war. A war against the Revolutionary oligarchs by Islamic Extremism. The appropriation of revolutionary discourse of the traditional Islamic discourse of Jihad to serve their purpose saw the maintenance of a sex differentiation of the fidai, where Muslim women are excluded under revolutionary discourse. This meant that their operations against the colonizer did not amount to actions of the fidai when they were killed in action. Revolutionary discourse insisted that the most acclaimed form of service to the Revolution was preserved for the male Muslim. This illustrates the operational alliance revolutionary discourse sought with traditional Islam to enable victory against French domination and in exerting hegemony over the free state of Algeria. Fanon returns to the relationship between the Muslim woman and the khimar as follows: "The veil covers the body and disciplines it, tempers it, at the very time when it experiences its phase of greatest effervescence. The veil protects, reassures, isolates." "to appreciate the importance of the veil for the body of the woman." "She has the anxious feeling that something is unfinished, and along with this a frightful sensation of disintegrating. The absence of the veil distorts the Algerian woman's corporal pattern, She quickly has to invent new dimensions for her body, new means of muscular control. She has to create for herself an attitude of unveiled woman-outside." (Fanon 1965 pg. 59). The khimar is then an instrument of power of traditional Islam, which symbolizes the power relations of traditional Islamic discourse, which define the terrain of being Muslim. To strip away the khimar is then to deconstruct the person constituted by traditional Islamic discourse, which is in fact a crisis of belief and definition of self in the world. The Muslim woman is then being called upon to make grave sacrifices of self that are not asked of Muslim men. A Muslim woman constituted as a fit and able Arab woman is called upon for the Revolution to willingly participate in actions which destroy her claim to be Muslim as they are haraam/forbidden in Islamic discourse, for the sake of the Revolution. It is being demanded of her that she destroy her claim to being Muslim and sever herself from a Muslim social order for the sake of Revolution. But the revolution offers no alternate validating Islamic discourse whilst it dances an opportunistic dance with traditional Islamic discourse, as traditional Islamic discourse invalidates and rejects her Muslim credentials. The Revolution offers the worship of the secular, absolute Revolution which is haraam for Muslims. The Revolution then is seeking the rejection of Islamic discourse and the embrace of pragmatic nihilism, which drives its oligarchs. Fanon continues: "The Algerian woman who walks stark naked into the European city relearns her body, establishes it in a totally revolutionary fashion. This new dialectic of the body and of the world is primary in the case of one revolutionary woman." (Fanon 1965 pg. 59). Deconstructed and freed of the limitations imposed by traditional Islam and its instrument of power, the khimar, the woman is constituted anew, with revolutionary discourse into a revolutionary women. But this new woman constituted by the revolution is a contradiction in terms, as so-called revolutionary discourse is dancing with traditional Islamic discourse to enable the dictatorship of the revolutionary oligarchs, driven by the quest for hegemonic power and wealth accumulation, to the detriment of the masses, whether revolutionary or not. This new revolutionary woman is constituted plagued with contradictions which enable the strategic intent of the revolutionary oligarchs and by extension the neo-colonial condition. This new revolutionary person riven with contradictions, in their quest for wholeness and healing, intensified by the failure of the revolution to deliver at the ground level, soon embraces Sunni Islamic extremism as the self-medication.

Fanon now extols the evolution of the khimar into an instrument of revolutionary war against the white colonizer. Fanon states: "The old fear of dishonor was swept away by a new fear, fresh and cold-that of death in battle or of torture of the girl. Behind the girl, the whole family-even the Algerian father, the authority of all things, the founder of every value-following in her footsteps, becomes committed to the new Algeria." (Fanon 1965 pg. 60). The revolution and the revolutionary woman has defined the role of the woman and brought patriarchy to heel, illustrated with the support of the revolution by the father. This absolute, that is revolution, is now the hegemonic absolute in the worldview of Algerians. The revolution now forced patriarchy to concede its hegemony over the woman but this revolutionary discourse refuses to name women who die in battle fidai/shahid or even admit them to the realm of recruits to the state of being fidai. Traditional Islam and its patriarchy is still alive and operational as revolutionary discourse is only seeking space to create its oligarchy and capture hegemonic power over the social order. The revolutionary women are then trapped in a schizophrenic discursive order.

Fanon continues: "Removed and re-assumed again and again, the veil has been manipulated, transformed into a technique of camouflage, into a means of struggle. The virtually taboo character assumed by the veil in the colonial situation disappeared almost entirely in the course of the liberating struggle." "There is thus a historic dynamism of the veil that is very concretely perceptible in the development of colonization in Algeria. In the beginning, the veil was a mechanism of resistance, but its value for the social group remained very strong. The veil was worn because tradition demanded a rigid separation of the sexes, but also because the occupier *was bent on unveiling Algeria*. In the second phase, the mutation occurred with the Revolution and under special circumstances. The veil was abandoned in the course of Revolutionary action. What had been used to block the psychological or political offensives of the occupier became a means, an instrument. The veil helped the Algerian woman to meet the new problems created by the struggle. The colonialists are incapable of grasping the motivations of the colonized. It is the necessities of combat that gives rise in Algerian society to new attitudes, to new modes of action, to new ways." (Fanon 1965 pgs. 63-64). The strategic definition of the khimar kept evolving in Algeria because of the power relations impacting the khimar with the colonizer. It is the colonizer that set the khimar in play with the colonized responding to the intent of the colonizer. The assault of the colonizer on the khimar demanded the formulation of a counter discourse, revolutionary discourse of the khimar, for the colonizer is seeking to define discursively the khimar as a weapon in their arsenal. In response the ambivalence at best of the revolutionary agents is glaring as they view the khimar as problematic, but cannot entertain alienating traditional Islam as it is vitally necessary to victory. This battle for hegemony will be postponed until freedom. The embrace of the revolution as absolute, masked with a veneer of traditional Islam, is the alternate discourse they hope will earn freedom and then hegemony over the free Algerian social order. This revolutionary discourse now embraces the khimar as an instrument in the war on the colonizer and a multifaceted strategy of the present war and the war to follow in a bid to disarm traditional Islam. Clearly, a strategy intent on stealing the Revolution and embracing the neo-colonial condition by a hegemonic, revolutionary oligarchy.

The text of Fanon ends with an article published on May 16, 1957 in Resistance Algerienne. Fanon is insisting, that the very basis of the daily life of the Muslim woman of Algeria under colonial domination, is the foundation of the revolutionary action the Muslim woman undertakes, in the war against French colonial domination. The wellspring of revolutionary action by the Algerian Muslim woman is then traditional Islam. Traditional Islam then constitutes fitting and able recruits for the Revolution, which means, that there is a symbiotic relationship between the two and eventually the Revolution will transform traditional Islam. We see clearly the pitfalls of Fanon's continued embrace of the white man's discourse of Enlightenment left-wing extremism. Fanon states: "To begin with, there is the much discussed status of the Algerian woman-her alleged confinement, her lack of importance, her humility, her silent existence based on quasi-absence. And 'Moslem society' has made no place for her, amputating her personality, allowing her neither development nor maturity, maintaining her in a perpetual infantilism." (Fanon 1965 pf. 65). This is the colonizer's discourse of Islam and the Muslim woman formulated to specifically assault the khimar towards destabilizing the Muslim social order of Algeria. Fanon now counters this white colonizer discourse with the revolutionary discourse of the symbiotic dynamism with traditional Islam. In speaking of the relationship between the family and the social order Fanon presents his revolutionary discourse. Fanon states: "The home is the basis of the truth of society, but society authenticates and legitimizes the family, The colonial structure is the very negation of this reciprocal justification. The Algerian woman, in imposing such a restriction on herself, in choosing a form of existence limited in scope, was deepening her consciousness of struggle and preparing for combat. This withdrawal, this rejection of an imposed structure, this falling back on the fertile kernel that a restricted but coherent existence represents, constituted for a long time the fundamental strength of the occupied. All alone, the woman, by means of conscious techniques, presided over the setting up of the system. What was essential was that the occupier should constantly come up against a united front. This accounts for the aspect of sclerosis that tradition must assume. In reality, the effervescence and the revolutionary spirit have been kept alive by the woman in the home. For revolutionary war is not a war of men." (Fanon 1965 pg. 66). Fanon's rationale then creates a symbiotic relationship between traditional Islam and

Revolutionary discourse. The Muslim woman accepted dutifully, her place assigned to her by traditional Islam, and actively moved to shore up the family, and by extension the social order, through the structurally crucial dual validation between the family and the social order, motivated only by her commitment to Islam. Traditional Islam then, through its discourse of purdah, facilitated the emergence of a proto-revolutionary Muslim woman, who accepted the task of shoring up the family, when the white colonizer severed and alienated the dual validation necessary between the family and the social order. By insulating the Muslim family from the assault of the white colonizer, this Muslim woman was then was an indispensable asset of the revolution, who then became a revolutionary soldier. This specific Muslim woman was the product of traditional Islam, then appropriated by the Revolution, thereby joining traditional Islamic discourse to Revolutionary discourse, in a white cosmology of the linear march of progress. Upon the removal of the colonizer with freedom won this discourse of Fanon has little relevance to the power relations of freedom. What it did was effectively mask the agenda of the revolutionary elite in their quest to manage Islam, towards attaining their hegemony over the masses. Fanon's discourse of the khimar/veil and revolution serves a Revolution which he believes to be an absolute, but it is of limited utility in visualizing the power relations of post-colonial Algeria. The euphoria of the success of the Revolution and the intoxication of the belief that it is an absolute, blinded visualization of the operational reality, that freedom will make greater and much more potent demands on the revolutionary elite. This elite responded to these demands with the application of colonial methodology to control and suppress the masses, thereby constituting the Algerian neo-colonial condition. Revolution does not and cannot as a talisman protect a people from the throttling of it by the elites, who then grow into an oligarchy. Revolution can never be an absolute, for it is never immune from power relations, both those of the colonial period and the period of freedom and the power relations of the anti-colonial struggle impact those of the period of freedom. Algeria today is the living testimony to this reality of power.

Chapter 2
Battling Discourses, radio and the Revolutionary

In this chapter Fanon analyses the nature of the discourse unleashed by Radio-Alger, the voice of the white colonizer broadcast to all of Algeria and the reaction of the Algerian to it. Fanon states: "We shall have occasion to show throughout this book that the challenging of the very principle of foreign domination brings about essential mutations in the consciousness of the colonized. In the manner in which he perceives the colonizer, in his human status in the world." (Fanon 1965 pg. 69). The challenge to and the rejection of the discourse of Radio-Alger was then a challenge to foreign domination which impacted the consciousness of the Algerian. This altered consciousness was now necessary to making the Revolution, made it possible and enabled it. Algerians as a result of colonial inequality simply could not afford to buy a radio receiver necessary for Radio-Alger to impact their consciousness. Others simply chose not to purchase a radio receiver as the discourse of Radio-Alger was at odds with the sensibilities of traditional Islam. But this reason given to those who asked why, masked the other aspect of the rejection, which was the discourse of Radio-Alger. Fanon states: "Radio-Alger is a confirmation of the settler's right and strengthens his certainty in the historic continuity of the conquest, hence of his farm." (Fanon 1965 pg. 71). "Among European farmers, the radio was broadly regarded as a link with the civilized world, as an effective instrument of resistance to the corrosive influence of an inert native society, of a society without a future, backward and devoid of value." (Fanon 1965 pg. 72). The discourse of Radio-Alger was formulated to maintain the solidarity of the white settler population in the face of the barbaric attack by the Arab hordes against modernity and progress available only through white supremacy. The white settlers must be continuously reminded of the reasons for the defense of French colonial domination in the 1950's in Algeria, which all involved the protection and hegemony of the white settlers over the Arab hordes. The discourse of Radio-Alger by extension was also meant for consumption by the non-whites laboring under hallucinatory whiteness, towards affirming the inherent superiority of white culture, the path to progress and modernity inherent only to white culture and affirming their embrace of white culture, their self-hate and their alienation from the Algerian masses. Radio-Alger and its discourse was never designed to entice the Algerian masses to embrace the culture of the French colonizer towards disarming the Revolution. Its primary task was to shore up the resolve of the white settlers to commit to the anti-Revolutionary war by not leaving Algeria for France, which would be a grave blow to the war effort. Fanon states: "*The radio in occupied Algeria is a technique in the hands of the occupier which, within the framework of colonial domination, corresponds to no vital need insofar as the 'native' is concerned.*" (Fanon 1965 pgs. 72-73). The technology of the radio has great unutilized potential for both antagonists in the war for Algeria. The French colonizer by choosing the specific discourse for radio ensures it is irrelevant to the daily life of the Algerian masses, thereby creating space for the revolutionary elite to now exploit this space for the purpose of mass mobilization in favor of the Revolution. Fanon continues: "The messages broadcast by Radio-Alger are listened to solely by the representatives of power in Algeria, solely by members of the dominant authority and seem magically to be avoided by the members of the 'native' society." (Fanon 1965 pg. 73). A most potent distinction between the colonial and neo-colonial condition which impacts the operational mechanisms of domination under the neo-colonial condition. Under the neo-colonial condition we are free. There are no occupiers and settlers, they are all here on our invitation. There is then no need to shore up a white settler population, which opens all vistas to be exploited to ensure North Atlantic/white supremacy. The digital communications revolution of the late twentieth and early twenty-first centuries has expanded decisively this space to be exploited under the neo-colonial condition so necessary to the hegemony of white supremacy. The neo-colonial condition is a preferred operational mode to that of colonial domination, from the mid-twentieth century until such time there arises non-white nations of the periphery capable of effectively challenging white supremacist hegemony over the world. At this instance the white world instinctively resorts to the mechanisms developed under white colonial domination. The French colonial occupier was intent on breaking the back of the Revolution only with military might and terror. Having lost Indochina to the Revolution they were now convinced that the issue's core was the unwillingness of the white, French colonial overlord to do what was militarily necessary to win the war against the Algerian rebels. The French colonial overlord saw no need for impacting the hearts and minds of an inferior race in rebellion, for this was totally ineffective and hence unnecessary, when dealing with an inferior colonized race, especially Arabs. White supremacist delusion viewed Algeria as theirs by right, by entitlement in the 1950's and as a result it is totally permissible to win victory over this inferior race by any means necessary. This is the same worldview of white supremacist hegemony in the 21st century where mass destruction is a plausible instrument of maintaining the hegemony of white supremacy over the world.

Fanon now deals with the pressure on the Algerian to walk away from the seclusion of traditional Islam and enter the worldview of the Revolution, which encompassed a range of ideas and realities demanding her/his knowledge of in order to become Revolution literate and functional. This operational terrain demanded access to news and ideas that countered those of the white occupier. The Revolutionary elite must now utilise a mass communication arm and the masses must acquire access to news, whether through the purchase of a radio receiver and reading the press of the Revolution. For Fanon, the Revolution inherited the resistance fostered by traditional Islam to white occupation, transforming it into Revolutionary resistance thereby unleashing this absolute on the Algerian masses. Fanon states: "From the first months of the Revolution the Algerian, with a view to self-protection and in order to escape what he considered to be the occupier's lying maneuvers, thus found himself having to acquire his own source of information. It became essential to know what was going on, to be informed of the enemy's real losses and his own. The Algerian had at this time to bring his life up to the level of the Revolution." "The Algerian's reaction was no longer that of pained and desperate refusal. *Because it avowed its own uneasiness, the occupier's lie became a positive aspect of the nation's new truth.*" (Fanon 1965 pg. 76). The Algerian was forced by the revolution to move from the position of refusal to one of informed action by the revolutionary elite through its dominance of the pipelines through which an alternate truth was peddled to the masses. With freedom this hegemony over the generation and dispersal of discourse to the masses by the

Revolutionary elite was protected with all the resources of this elite, as its hegemony was vital to the quest for the formation and hegemony of the revolutionary oligarchs.

Fanon makes a passing statement on the impact of the Revolution on the mind and actions of the colonizer and the colonized. The impact of the Revolution on the mental health of the colonizer was different from that of the colonized, which illustrates the nature of the extremist tendencies of white supremacist discourse when its hegemony is challenged by inferior races. Fanon states: "The European became aware of the fact that the life he had built on the agony of the colonized people was losing its assurance." "In the dominant group, likewise, there were cases of mental hysteria, people would be seized with a collective fear and panicky settlers were keen to seek an outlet in criminal acts. What made the two cases was that, unlike the colonized, the colonizer, always translated his subjective state into acts, real and multiple murders." (Fanon 1965 pg. 79). When faced with what they considered an existential threat posed to their hegemony by an inferior race, white supremacists are hard wired by their discourse and its attendant worldview to apply genocide as their instrument of the apocalypse.

Fanon returns to his presentation on news and the Algerian Revolution by stating the relationship that developed between the producer and broadcaster of Revolutionary news and the Algerian masses, which indicated the existence of the means within the strategy of the anti-colonial revolution to enable hi-jacking of the Revolution by the elite. Fanon states: "In Algeria, on the contrary-all the news is good, every bit is gratifying. The Fifth Column is an impossibility in Algeria." "These manifestations, these attitudes of total belief, this collective conviction, express the determination of the group to get as close as possible to the Revolution, to get ahead of the Revolution if possible, in short *to be in on it*." (Fanon 1965 pg. 80). The masses were then the captives of the revolutionary elite at the level of the idea, thereby enabling the formation and hegemony of the Revolutionary oligarchy from its revolutionary elite. The very course of the Revolution and the power relations between the masses and the revolutionary elite enabled the drive to evolve from a revolutionary elite to a hegemonic oligarchy to the detriment of the masses. The illiteracy of the masses in French meant that colonial literature in French was alien to the masses. Given the embrace of French by the revolutionary elite, the problem also applied to their literature in French, hence the need for the masses to acquire radios to access the vocal message of the revolutionary elite in a language the masses were comfortable with. At this stage of the Revolution the chasm which separated the revolutionary elite from grounding with the masses was its hallucinatory whiteness. With freedom it was inevitable that the revolutionary elite would move to insulate themselves as a hegemonic oligarchy from the masses. Fanon states: "It must not be forgotten that the people's generalized illiteracy left it indifferent to things written. In the first months of the Revolution, the great majority of Algerians identified everything written in the French language as the expression of colonial domination." (Fanon 1965 pg. 82). Were the masses illiterate in Quranic Arabic, thereby unable to read the Quran? The rejection of French as the language of the colonizer by the masses then dealt a blow to the bias for French as the language of the Revolutionary elite. The revolutionary elite was forced then by the realities of the masses to now communicate with them on the terms set by the masses. This intensified the resolve of the revolutionary elite to distinguish themselves from the masses whilst wielding hegemonic power over them. The masses then led the way with their embrace of radio as the means to connect with the Revolutionary elite through its radio service in a language rooted in a cultural framework acceptable to them. It is then by utilizing radio the revolutionary elite propagated its discourse of revolutionary Jihad against the French colonizer for the liberation of Algeria to the masses. Fanon states: "since 1956 the purchase of a radio in Algeria has meant, not the adoption of a modern technique for getting news, but the obtaining of access of the only means of entering into communication with the Revolution, of living with it." (Fanon 1965 pg. 83). The masses made the decision to purchase the radio receivers as they were necessary to becoming organic to the Revolution. This drive for revolutionary participation then brought out the ingenuity of the masses to surmount the obstacles presented between their living conditions and the operational requirements for the radio receivers. Namely, the chronic lack of electrification in the communities of the Algerian masses and the means devised to overcome this shortfall such as receivers connected to batteries, even though not so designed by the manufacturer. Radio broadcasts in the pursuit of the

Revolution intensified the mass support of and action for the Revolution, degrading the power of the occupier, heightening that of the Revolution whilst boosting the power of the revolutionary elite over the masses through the dependency of the masses at the level of the idea on the revolutionary elite. Fanon states: "In making of the radio a primary means of resisting the increasingly overwhelmingly psychological and military pressures of the occupant, Algerian society made an autonomous decision to embrace the new technique and thus tune itself in on the new signaling systems brought into being by the Revolution. The Voice of Fighting Algeria was to be of capital importance in consolidating and unifying the people. We shall see that the use of Arab, Kabyle and French languages which, as colonialism was obliged to recognize, was the expression of a non-racial conception," (Fanon 1965 pg. 84). The motivation of the masses to embrace the Revolution demanded communication with the masses that affirmed their daily existential reality, not the exploitation of its limitations imposed by white colonial domination. The revolutionary elite was forced to communicate in the languages of the masses, whilst insisting that it was necessary to broadcast in French as an expression of the elite's hallucinatory whiteness and their quest for the embrace and affirmation of the colonizing race. Under the assault of the white colonizer, the revolutionary elite made all public attempts at signifying their embrace and practice of universalist principles towards the erasure of all forms of tensions within the masses that divided the masses. With freedom, the revolutionary elite spared no effort to enhance these tensions to divide the masses necessary to the hegemony of the revolutionary oligarchy.

Fanon presents his discourse of the transformation of French into the language of the Revolution. A discursive position which reveals Fanon's hallucinatory whiteness and his support for the agenda of the revolutionary elite, for he was an operational part of that elite. The revolutionary elite persisted in its embrace of French language as its preferred language of the Revolution, apparently much more immersed in white myth than the colonizers themselves. The intent was clear to suppress the languages of the masses through the preference for French language, the language of the colonized Algerian elite. It was also arrogant to believe that you can take the language of the colonizer and redefine it to serve the colonized, when the language retains its white supremacist discursive basis. For to remove its white supremacist core it is no longer French language but just words and certainly not French language befitting for the revolutionary elite. This embrace of French language was the message to the masses that they must now embrace revolutionary culture expressed with French language, jettisoning their native discourses, worldviews and culture. The revolutionary elite was intent on accomplishing what the white French colonizer failed to do, i.e. – extinguishing native culture. The embrace and retention of French language by the revolutionary elite meant that the basis for the neo-colonial condition at the level of the idea was now intact, within the French language and expressed via the French language. Fanon states: "The French language lost its accursed character, revealing itself to be capable also of transmitting, for the benefit of the nation, the message of truth that the latter awaited. Paradoxically as it may appear, it is the Algerian Revolution, it is the struggle of the Algerian people, that is facilitating the spreading of the French language in the nation." (Fanon 1965 pgs. 89-90). The revolutionary elite established its operational links to traditional Islam specifically illustrated in its use of the discourse of Jihad and the Shahid. Then through radio it deploys its strategy of using the French language as a language of communication with the masses in its strategy to have the French language become the dominant language of revolutionary Algeria. To embrace and deploy this strategy reveals the contempt for mass culture and the threat it poses to the revolutionary elite's agenda for hegemony of a revolutionary oligarchy. Fanon continues as follows: "Used by the *Voice of the Combatants*, conveying in a positive way the message of the Revolution, the French language also becomes an instrument of liberation. Whereas formerly, in psychopathology, any French voice, to one in a delirium, expressed rejection, condemnation and opprobrium, with the struggle for liberation we see the initiation of a major process of exorcising the French language. The 'native' can almost be said to assume responsibility for the language of the occupier." (Fanon 1965 pg. 90). The choice made by the revolutionary elite to broadcast to the masses in French language was deliberate and had nothing to do with re-constituting the French language into the language of the Revolution. It was to preserve the French language as the language of the dominant, hegemonic revolutionary oligarchy, where the revolutionary social order was premised on the French language retaining its hegemonic position of Logos, the hegemonic word. The colonial/neo-colonial continuum in Algeria was then premised on the retention of the French language as Logos. Under the Revolution the masses were then called upon to embrace the French language and successive generations of the Revolution were educated with the French language as Logos. At the level of the idea, where the masses lost control of the Revolution, it was expressed in the French language not in the languages of the masses before colonial domination. The revolutionary elite with freedom continued to play its game with traditional Islam by insisting that Arabic was the official language of revolutionary Algeria, whilst the French language remains the Logos to the oligarchy. This is reflected in the reality that under the revolution the French language has been embraced by successive generations of Algerians as their second language. Fanon states: "It is the intervention of the foreign nation that puts order into the original anarchy of the colonized country. Under these conditions, the French language, the language of the occupier, was given the role of *Logos*, with ontology implications within Algerian society." (Fanon 1965 pg. 91). The colonizer insisted that the hegemony of the French language, of French language as Logos was necessary towards unifying diverse Algeria into a whole, a totality. The revolutionary elite personally accepted the French language as Logos for the very discursive constructs that drove their revolutionary worldview were validated, affirmed and made real by the French language, The Logos. Arabic, especially Quranic Arabic did not do the necessary for the revolutionary elite, neither did Arabic dialect and the other languages of Algeria, but the dance must continue with traditional Islam. The revolutionary elite define themselves by the French language, the Logos that they made their instrument of oligarchic hegemony. This Logos under the revolution continues to impact the ontology of the Algerian constituting the neo-colonial condition and its various manifestations. Fanon insists that the product of the revolution was the Arabic language divorced from the Quran, a secularized language serving the revolution and French language defined to serve the revolution, not the white colonizer. But he fails to deal with the quest for hegemony between both languages in the new Algeria, one being the language of the masses, namely Arabic, and French language the Logos that defines the revolutionary project of the revolutionary elite. This battle is ongoing to this day in Algeria. Fanon states: "In August 1956, the reality of combat and the confusion of the occupier stripped the Arabic language of its sacred character, and the French language of its negative connotation. The new language of the nation could then make itself known through multiple meaningful channels." (Fanon 1965 pg. 92). For Fanon secularized Arabic and revolutionary French were now the two major languages contending for hegemony in revolutionary Algeria, despite the reality that French language literacy in no way posed a challenge to Arabic dominance when Fanon wrote. Fanon was then expressing a desire, wish, hope and expectation of his which subsequently the revolutionary oligarchy is still actively seeking to accomplish. The revolutionary elite utilized the traditional Islamic discourse of Jihad and the Shahid to justify, win support and mobilize the Algerian masses for the Revolution. This meant that the Revolution did not have the means to secularize Arabic and the tensions created remained present and active until the 1990's when Islam became the viable alternative to the revolutionary oligarchy in general elections, who responded as all oligarchs do with brutal repression and violence against the masses. The masses had now embraced Islam as the new form of the Revolution and paid for it with their blood. Arabic was then never secularized by the Revolution, as it was incapable of so doing given its use of Islamic discourse to legitimize the Revolution.

As Fanon ends this chapter of his work he returns to the role of the radio in the Revolution and its future role in building a free nation. Fanon states: "What we have witnessed is a radical transformation of the means of perception, of the very world of perception. *The Voice of Algeria* created out of nothing, brought the nation to life and endowed every citizen with a new status, *telling him so explicitly*." (Fanon 1965 pg. 96). The discourse of the Revolution dispersed through the radio deeply impacted the colonized Algerian for it changed the structure of and the methodology of native perception, the colonized Algerian. The Logos of the Revolutionary elite, the vanguard, willed into being the new ontology of the free, Revolutionary Algerian. This vanguard is the Logos of the Revolution and to reject this Logos is counter-revolution, necessitating the defense of the Revolution by any means necessary. The Logos eminently qualified to rule does so through the oligarchy that it constitutes for its own protection, aggrandizement and wealth accumulation. The revolutionary power of the masses must always be an empty mobilization instrument of the vanguard, for the masses can never be allowed to grasp and exert power. Fanon states in ending the chapter as follows: "After the war a disparity between the people and what is intended to speak for them will no longer be possible." "The identification of the voice of the Revolution with the fundamental truth of the nation has opened limitless horizons." (Fanon 1965 pg. 97). Fanon again slips into denial mode at best, when arising from his embrace of the white enlightenment concept of the Revolution as absolute he insists that there can be no power relation between the masses and the discourse that speaks for the people and to the people. The only instrument that erases the power relation that develops from within the Revolution, between the vanguard and its discursive agents, who always seek to exert hegemony over the masses at the level of the idea, is for the masses to develop their own discursive agents formulating discourse in their favor. A revolutionary vanguard intent on growing into a hegemonic revolutionary oligarchy, from the outset of the rebellion against the white colonizer jealously guarded its right to define the discourse of the anti-colonial war and post-colonial nation. The Voice of the Revolution then was charged with propagating the discourse of truth of the nation formulated by the discursive agents of the Revolutionary vanguard for the personal benefit of the vanguard, to the exclusion of the masses. Exerting hegemony through the instruments of power of the discourse of truth of the nation over the masses of Algeria opened limitless horizons only for the revolutionary vanguard for so it was designed to achieve, for the masses there was only patronage and suppression followed by brazen brutality when necessary. This then is Algeria's neo-colonial condition because of and in spite of its successful anti-colonial war of liberation. The Revolution in itself cannot immunize the free nation which emerges from the power relations that constitute the neo-colonial condition; as the Revolution was never intent on enabling the masses to wield power at the ground level of the matrices of power in post-colonial Algeria.

Chapter 3
The Family and the Revolution

Fanon in this chapter of his work presents his analysis of the impact of the Revolution on the Algerian family constituted by traditional Islam. Fanon insists that it was the embrace of the woman and the khimar/veil as instruments of the Revolution that impacted the traditional family form, thereby commencing the transformative process. Fanon states: "We have seen the transformation of the Algerian woman taking place through her revolutionary commitment and her instrumentalisation of the veil. It will be readily understood that this radical change could not occur without having profound repercussions on the other components of Algerian family life." (Fanon 1965 pg. 99). The embrace of the Revolution and the commitment of the Algerian women to the strategy of the deployment of the woman in the revolutionary war, deeply impacted the Algerian family form under colonial domination. The Algerian woman immersed in the Revolution was the dynamic for change that forever changed the nature of the Algerian family during the war of liberation. Fanon defines his task in this chapter as follows: "We would like here to trace the evolution of the Algerian family, its transformation, the great modifications it has undergone because of and in the course of the war for liberation." (Fanon 1965 pg. 99). The war for liberation, specifically the strategy of this war has deeply impacted the Algerian family form. The nature of this impact Fanon describes as follows: "The most important point of this modification, it seems to us, is that the family, from being homogeneous and virtually monolithic, has broken up into separate elements. Each member of this family has gained in individuality what it has lost in its belonging to a world of more or less confused values. Individual persons have found themselves facing new choices, new decisions. The customary and highly structured patterns of behavior that were crystallizations of traditional ideas suddenly proved ineffective and were abandoned. Tradition, in fact, is not solely a combination of automatic gestures and archaic beliefs. At the most elementary level, there are values, and the need for justification. The father questioned by the child explains, comments, legitimizes." (Fanon 1965 pgs. 99-100). The homogeneous family, with the woman in her specific place, was for all intents and purposes a monolith premised on male hegemony rooted in traditional Islam. The strategy of the war for liberation for the woman cracked this homogeneous operational monolith by enabling and encouraging individualism of genders, age groups and generations bound by the family. The father and the power wielded by the father was under assault from the war of liberation as his children were all now infused by the individualism generated by the war for liberation. The hegemony of the father in the family was the product of tradition, specifically traditional Islam, which meant that the war for liberation in collapsing the power of tradition in the family was assaulting the hegemony of traditional Islam. This individualism was the product of and the indication of the collapse of the power of traditional Islam which meant that members of families so impacted were now in a state of anomie. As the family form was under question, the power of the father was assailed but the alternative family life was still a work in progress as crucial questions were yet to be answered. In this context where a war for liberation is being fought whilst members of the traditional family form are seeking answers to questions and intent on making decisions, whilst their ties to the past are under question. The Revolutionary elite is charged with the task of providing such answers and knowledge necessary to form a new family form, but what they offer is a drastic severance from the past, whilst utilizing the symbolism of the past to mobilize mass participation and a cult of the Revolution as absolute, which insists on belief driven by revolutionary fervor or blind faith, which is haraam under Islamic discourse. The Revolution then is offering ambivalence at best, colonial/post-colonial bi-polarity or schizophrenia at worst, as the solution to the anomie generated by the war for liberation. The enemy to be defeated was not the colonial occupier but Islam, as the only viable, alternate discourse to the discourse of the Revolution was Islamic discourse. Fanon now writes on the preservation of the traditional family form and the hegemony of the father in the absence of the war for liberation. The launch of the war for liberation changed the dynamics of the family form internally and its dependent relationship with colonial occupation, which facilitated and enabled the hegemony of the father. The traditional family form as traditional Islam was then a satellite of the colonial occupier and her/his discourse of white supremacy. Fanon states: "It is important to show that the colonized father at the time of the fight for liberation gave his children the impression of being undecided, of avoiding the taking of sides, even of adopting an evasive and irresponsible attitude." (Fanon 1965 pg. 100). Faced with the reality of the war for liberation, the father was at best vacillating in expressing to the family his position on the role the family must play in reference to the war of liberation. The members of the family, especially the children of the family of fighting age, were now forced into a state of anomie by the clash between the war for liberation and the father who was providing no leadership. The Revolution then intervened and relieved the crisis of identity and purpose plaguing the members of the family by displacing the authority of the father with that of the Revolution. The Revolution solved the problem of the recalcitrant father wielding power against the wishes of the Revolution, by first generating the anomie and then resolving it, thereby breaking the back of the power of the father in the family form, replacing it with the power of the Revolutionary elite and the State it commands, especially with freedom. This is supposedly a benevolent transfer of power in the family form which subsequently revealed itself to be simply an instrument of the power of the revolutionary oligarchy. Fanon is insisting that the centrality of the power of the father in the family form was unchallenged by the assault on the Algerian family form and the members of the family by colonial domination. For Fanon, there was a symbiotic relationship between colonial domination and the power of the father, where the power of the father provided a safe haven for the assault of colonial domination on the personality and on the family form of the colonized. The only way to break this symbiotic relationship was through Revolutionary action which assaulted the power of the father in the family simultaneously with the assault on white colonial domination and the personality of the colonized constituted with domination. Fanon states: "The conqueror had settled in such numbers, he had created so many centers of colonization, that a certain passivity encouraged by the colonial domination made itself evident and gradually took on a tinge of despair. Before 1954, the son who adopted a nationalist position never did so, really, against the father's wishes, but his activity as a militant in any case never in any respect modified his filial behavior within the framework of the Algerian family. The relations based on the absolute respect due to the father and on the principle that the truth is first of all unchallengeable property of the elders were not encroached upon. Modesty, shame, the fear of looking at the father, of speaking aloud in his presence, remained intact, even in the case of the nationalist militants. The absence of actual revolutionary action kept the personality in its customary channels." (Fanon 1965 pgs. 100-101). The centrality of the power of the father in the family was potent and extensive to the extent where the commitment to nationalist militant anti-colonial politics by members of the family, especially the sons, did not challenge nor erode the power of the father. The father conceptualized under traditional Islamic discourse was an instrument of colonial domination effectively ensuring passivity of the Algerian family, that grew into despair. The power of the father must be destroyed as is the case with colonial discourse as they are both joined at the hips, but the only effective means to do so is revolutionary action, anti-colonial violence. Fanon continues on this theme of the cleansing nature of revolutionary action/violence as follows: "In a parallel way, his attitude toward his father and the other members of the family frees itself of everything that proves unnecessary and detrimental to the revolutionary situation. The person is born, assumes his autonomy, and becomes the creator of his own values. The old stultifying attachments to the father melts in the sun of the Revolution." (Fanon 1965 pg. 101). This Revolutionary action destroys the power of the father, frees the child of the despair constituted by colonial domination and traditional Islam, with the product being an Algerian person freed of all encumbrances constituted by colonial domination and traditional Islam. This new person is then anomic and in dire need of a new discourse with its attendant worldview that addresses the void created by revolutionary action. This was the task of the revolutionary elite and they set about the task by formulating a discourse that suited their desire for hegemony. Hence the potent challenge posed by Islam in the 1990's to the hegemony of the revolutionary oligarchy for they failed, as Fanon did, to recognize the place of Islamic discourse in the construct of the worldview of the Algerian in the post-colonial revolutionary social order of the 1950's and 1960's. This inability is potently illustrated by this statement of Fanon: "The group, which formerly looked to the father to determine its values, now had to seek these each for himself, as circumstances dictated." (Fanon 1965 pg. 102). The power of the father was under constant questioning from Islamic discourse, hence the need for a male power structure to police male dominance in a persistent effort to silence Islamic discourse. White colonial domination, with its paranoia over the threat posed by Islamic discourse, enhanced the power of the father in the family with its assault on Islamic discourse thereby laying the foundation of the symbiotic relationship with male power in the social order. In her/his anomic condition the individual has a range of choices now available under revolutionary conditions, namely Revolutionary and Islamic discourses. The Revolution then liberated Islamic discourse from the restrictions placed on its evolutionary adaptability to daily life and demands placed on it by traditional Islam and its dance with colonial domination. This evolutionary resurgence of Islamic discourse is confirmed by the events of the 1990's in Algeria.

Fanon now deals specifically with the power relation between the son and the father in the context of colonial domination and the rupture unleashed by revolutionary action. Fanon states: "At the time when the people were called upon to adopt radical forms of struggle, the Algerian family was still highly structured. But on the level of national consciousness, the father lagged far behind the son." "Before the Revolution, which abruptly split the world in two, the father found himself disarmed and a little anxious." (Fanon 1965 pg. 102). The father was rooted in the traditional past in its subservience to colonial domination, whilst the son embraced the Revolution and became the instrument of power of the Revolution in the family, when the Revolution scorched the power base of the father via revolutionary action. The father was now forced to follow the lead of the son, thereby overturning the traditional order in its servility to colonial domination. Fanon insists that the father did not surrender and accept the new power relations spawned by the Revolution as there was resistance through the creation of a new operational mode in an attempt to keep the traditional order effective under the new reality. Fanon states: "The conversion of the father, however, did not totally eliminate traditional patterns of behavior. It was difficult for the father to stifle both his desire to re-establish his collapsed sovereignty and his obsession with the frightful consequences of this open war. Thus new forms of paternal opposition, veiled manifestations of paternal authority, came into light." (Fanon 1965 pg. 104). The push back from traditional Islam was expected, but the son immersed in the new power relation was in a state of anomie which necessitated an existing, cogent discourse of the Revolution to counter the move by traditional Islam. Instead, the Revolution injected ambivalence at best into the power relation with its dance with traditional Islam to win affirmation for its anti-colonial war and to legitimize the great sacrifices the masses were being called upon to make and the subsequent brutality unleashed on them by the colonizer. Traditional Islam survived, evolved and bided its time until the 1990's where it made its bid for power, with the widespread support of the masses through constitutional means, namely the electoral process. The revolutionary oligarchy responded as expected when faced with a constitutional loss of power, thereby making space for Salafi-Jihadi Sunni Islam to now engage militarily with the revolutionary oligarchy for power. The anomic condition constituted by the Revolution was never fully addressed by the Revolution, thereby granting space to traditional Islam to evolve into distinct forms potently indicating the organic failure of the Revolution in its post-colonial incarnation to exercise hegemony over the hearts and minds of

the Algerian people. This anomic condition today in the 21st century remains unaddressed as the protagonists in the battle for hegemony are organically unable to so do. Fanon states: "This defeat of the father by the new forces that were emerging could not fail to modify the relations that had formerly prevailed in Algerian society." (Fanon 1965 pg. 105). The power relations of the family were impacted and modified by the Revolution, but the father was not defeated as there was change, reformulation and response in an ongoing engagement to preserve the hegemony of the father/male in the family. The old order was finished but a new fluid order was in the making intent on creating an alternate order to that of the Revolution. And as it became clearer that the Revolutionary order was premised on the hegemony of a revolutionary oligarchy, the alternate order grew in strength as the masses embraced this alternate order in a quest to self-medicate themselves to cure the ravages of their persistent anomic condition.

Fanon now deals with the power relation between the daughter and the father and the impact of the Revolution on this power relation. The father was an instrument of power under traditional Islam to control the female, especially her sexual potential, which when not managed brought dishonor to the family, especially the father and other males of the family. The gravity of the changes to this power relation were then much more decisive that that of the father/son power relation. The anomic condition of the woman/daughter who embraced revolutionary action in the post-colonial revolutionary social order was much more pressing than that of the male/son with reference to the father/family. Fanon states: "All these restrictions were to be knocked over and challenged by the national liberation struggle. The unveiled Algerian woman, who assumed an increasingly important place in revolutionary action, developed her personality, discovered the existing realm of responsibility. The freedom of the Algerian people from then on became identified with woman's liberation, with her entry into history. This woman who, could not put herself back into her former state of mind and relive her behavior of the past; this woman who was writing the heroic pages of Algerian history was, in so doing, bursting the bounds of the narrow world in which she had lived without responsibility, and was at the same time participating in the destruction of colonialism and in the birth of the new woman." (Fanon 1965 pg. 107). In the war for liberation the drive to defeat the colonizer placed the power relation between father and daughter in stasis for a future date for resolution. But this was specifically those daughters who embraced revolutionary action, who were a minority in the population of female Algerians. With victory the power relation became fixated on the role of these female revolutionary veterans of war and space afforded them by the revolutionary elite. The revolutionary elite was and is dominated by males and the post-colonial social order remains focused on the male, which illustrates the dance of the revolutionary male elite with traditional Islam. The overwhelming majority of woman who were not revolutionary fighters found themselves faced with choices of a possible range of actions to be made that would impact their daily life and their standing in the community and social order. The reformulation and evolution of the discourse of traditional Islam ensured that pressures were constantly brought to bear on women in the post-colonial system to shoulder the burdens placed on them by their sex, yet still able to pursue their education, career etc. This was an accommodation between traditional Islam and the revolutionary elite/ oligarchy, where the common intent was to ensure that males wielded hegemonic power over females. The female revolutionary fighters were then an aberration effectively marginalized by both the revolutionary elite and traditional Islam, effectively immersing them in the intense anomie that plagued the Algerian female as a result of her revolutionary action. The revolutionary elite then betrayed these fighters, sacrificed on the altar of their expediency driven by their quest for hegemonic power. With demobilization following victory they returned to their families, or what was left of them, and communities where the push to re-establish the hegemony of male power was apparent. In this personal war, time was a potent enemy as there were no new fighting women being produced, the war was over hence the pressure to return to what was the norm. A visible minority, they then became relics of a revolutionary past as the present did not exalt them as the hegemonic model of the ideal Algerian female, plagued with their anomie, post-traumatic stress disorder, other psychological problems and physical incapacities of war. Fanon speaks only to what he saw as the reality of the revolutionary war against the colonizer, but the grinding reality of the social order after victory becomes the prime concern with victory. Algeria today then falsifies the belief that the course of the revolution against the colonizer determines the nature of the social order thereafter. The power relations of the post-colonial situation created Algeria today, power relations which indicate that Revolution is not an absolute. Fanon continues with his description of the product of the absolute that is Revolution as follows: "The women were no longer silent. Algerian society in the fight for liberation, in the sacrifices that it was willing to make in order to liberate itself from colonialism, renewed itself and developed new values governing sexual relations. The woman ceased to be a complement for man. *She literally forged a new place for herself by her sheer strength.*" "Old values, sterile and infantile phobias disappeared." (Fanon 1965 pgs. 109-110). Fanon is presenting his position on the transformation that took place amongst the revolutionary fighters engaged in a war for liberation against the colonizer. With the colonizer defeated and absent from Algeria a whole new order of power relations emerged, which potently illustrated that Fanon's much vaunted new values and the new woman were not deeply rooted in the social order, not even within the revolutionary elite, hence the condition of the masses in Algeria today. All that is necessary will be embraced by the revolutionary forces to defeat the colonizer, with freedom won another dimension of daily reality emerges which challenges the hegemony of the values of the revolutionary forces. What was considered necessary and tolerable under the exigencies of war against the colonizer, in post-colonial reality is challenged in the enduring battles to establish a new hegemonic order of power. A fundamental battle in this post-colonial war for hegemony was the power relations between the sexes.

Fanon now writes on the revolutionary couple involved in the revolutionary forces waging war on the colonizer. In this Fanon presents his model of the ideal couple, the foundation of modern, revolutionary, free Algeria. Fanon states: "The Algerian couple, in becoming a link in the revolutionary organization, is transformed into a unit of existence. The mingling of fighting experience with conjugal life deepens the relations between husband and wife and cements their union. There is a simultaneous and effervescent emergence of the citizen, the patriot, and the modern spouse. The Algerian couple rids itself of its traditional weaknesses at the same time that the solidarity of the people becomes a part of history." (Fanon 1965 pg. 114). Fanon's ideal couple is a minority in the social order of Algeria, with the salient question being if such ideal couples exist within the revolutionary elite. Did the revolutionary elite consist of, and constitute ideal males, females and couples that Fanon insists were the compulsory product of Revolutionary action against the colonizer? If yes, then they were effectively purged given the reality of the revolutionary oligarchy of Algeria that with victory hijacked the revolution. These revolutionary ideal couples of Fanon, always placed in a minority position within the population of Algeria, were soon faced with hard choices to be made as they were under the discipline of the revolutionary elite that grew into an oligarchy. Silence, obedience and feeding off of state patronage or resistance, marginalization, repression and murder. Then there was the ultimate coping mechanism invented under colonial domination and refurbished for post-colonial Algeria: ambivalence, pragmatic nihilism, nihilism/ self-destruction. The ideal male, female and couple of Fanon then became zombies, a living nightmare, castaways in a revolution they made.

Fanon now states his position on the changes brought to marriage and divorce practices of traditional Islam by the pragmatic response of the revolutionary agents of both sexes to the operational conditions they found themselves in, during the war against the colonizer. Fanon states: "Marriage in the maquis ceased to be an arrangement between families. All unions were voluntary. The future wife and husband had had time to know each other, to esteem, to love each other." "When the father learned of the marriage of his daughter in the maquis, the act would not be contested or condemned." (Fanon 1965 pg. 115). The Revolution had disarmed the order of traditional Islam through the generation of a war for liberation that rendered the old order inapplicable to the daily life of the revolutionary fighters against colonial domination. The new institutional order created in the crucible of war was then the brave, new world of the Revolution. But in Fanon's description of this new order for the new Algeria he illustrates the dance of revolutionary discourse with the traditional Islamic discourse of Jihad, where the revolutionary elite was portraying themselves as Muslims undertaking Jihad for the liberation of Algeria from the colonial domination of the crusaders. There was then no discursive break between revolutionary discourse and traditional Islamic discourse on the ground, in the imagery of the masses. Fanon states: "Marriage in Algeria underwent the radical transformation in the very heart of the combat waged by the *Moudjahidines* and the Moudjahidates." (Fanon 1965 pg. 116). The description used by Fanon of the male and female fighters of the Revolution are derivatives of the Quranic Arabic verb JAHID from the root JHD, used in the Islamic jurisprudence of Jihad, which describes the condition of being Muslim engaged in struggle for the sake of Islam, the product of being in total subjection to Almighty Allah (swt) to the point of death of the Muslim. The death of the Muslim was then only for Almighty Allah (swt) not for man, nor for a free Algeria, much less for a revolutionary elite. The use of the jurisprudence of Jihad by revolutionary discourse as seen in the case of Fanon's writings on Algeria meant, in fact, that the revolutionary elite was using Islamic discourse to win the support of the masses and to mobilize the masses. During the anti-colonial war revolutionary discourse failed to articulate to the masses its discourse of Islam, power and the social order in a revolutionary, free Algeria. But the use of the discourse of Islam at war conjured up images of the free, revolutionary Algeria that were discordant with that of the revolutionary elite. Hence the post-colonial embrace of colonial instruments of power by the revolutionary elite.

Fanon now writes on the price paid by the women of Algeria, especially women in the rural areas of Algeria, where the majority of the population resided. The ferocity of the violence unleashed by the colonizer on the rural social order changed it forever as no one could put humpty dumpty back together again. Fanon states: "Feminine society undergoes change both through an organic solidarity with the Revolution, and more especially because the adversary cuts into the Algerian flesh with unheard of violence." (Fanon 1965 pg. 116). Fanon insists that deliberately planned and orchestrated colonial violence, to break the back of the resistance to French colonial domination, has changed the very cultural fabric and the worldview of the Algerian recipient of this violence. In his description of this reality Fanon presents a scenario that can only be fully understood and experienced by a Muslim. Fanon states: "One does not weep, one does not do as before when one is faced with multiple murders. One grits one's teeth and one prays in silence. One further step, and it is cries of joy that salute the death of a moudjahid who has fallen on the field of honor." "The war has dislocated Algerian society to such a point that any death is conceived of as a direct or indirect consequence of colonialist repression." (Fanon 1965 pg. 118). Fanon is in fact describing a Muslim interpretation and imagery of war in the defense of Islam against Kaffirun/unbelievers/ invaders of a Muslim land. This description is in no way articulating a revolutionary war against a colonizer for the birth of a free nation, as it is not a product of Islamic discourse and its attendant worldview. The barbarity of the French assault has forced the Muslims, especially of rural Algeria, to live the life of Jihad hence to embrace and adopt the methodology of Jihad. The colonizer/ the Kaffirun is the cause of death of Muslims, there is no hope of peace with the Kaffirun which assures the survival of the Muslims under assault. Faced with Muslim genocide as a daily reality, there is only one possible Islamic/Muslim response: Jihad and its attendant discourse of the Shahid, the Islamic martyr. The soldier of Jihad, the moudjahid willingly embraces martyrdom, of being Shahid. In this condition of peril, where Jihad is the only viable solution, the Muslim becomes immersed in the discourse of war, the honoring of the moudjahid and the shahid as the role models constituted by Islamic discourse for this condition of disorder and the return to normalcy premised on Islamic hegemony. The question that arises is: if this Muslim interpretation of the war against the colonizer saw the revolutionary elite as Muslims undertaking Jihad as the Muslims' obligation to Almighty Allah (swt)? The masses of Algeria indicated their assessment of the revolutionary elite, now an oligarchy, in the 1990's.

The spectrum of trauma unleashed on the Algerian and the Algerian family deeply impacted the worldview that defined the operational basis of the family. The salient issue presented by analysis of this impact and the worldview of action that emerged which drove Algerian action against white colonial domination remains the product of the eye of the beholder. For Fanon this Algerian revolutionary action was not the product of an Islamic worldview but that of the absolute of Revolution; where the reality on the ground was much more complex than that presented by Fanon and those who are believers in the absolute of Revolution. This complexity was potently illustrated by the complexity of the worldview of the masses in the 1990s with their search and support for an alternative political discourse to that of the revolutionary oligarchy.

Chapter 4
Western Medicine as an Instrument of Colonial Power

Fanon analyses the use of western medicine to exert French, white colonial, power over the Algerian, where in the spaces dominated by western medicine the Algerian seeking medical care is primarily subjected to white, colonial domination with medical care as the afterthought. The Algerian reacts to western medical spaces as she/he reacts to other colonial spaces, for the experience of being in a colonial medical space is no different from other colonial spaces. There is then an Algerian expectation that conditions their very choice to enter this colonial medical space and their behavior whilst within the space. Fanon states: "Introduced into Algeria at the same time as racialism and humiliation, Western medical science, being part of the oppressive system, has always provoked in the native an ambivalent attitude. This ambivalence is in fact to be found in connection with all of the occupier's modes of presence. With medicine we come to one of the most tragic features of the colonial situation." (Fanon 1965 pg. 121). The colonized Algerian responds to colonial domination with ambivalence, as other colonized peoples, but ambivalence continues as the common response of the masses to the State and the social order of the post-colonial, free nation, which indicates that domination mirroring the nature of colonial domination now continues under the post-colonial/neo-colonial condition. In the neo-colonial condition the instruments of power mirror those of the colonial order, but there is no white colonizer exerting power as citizens of the free nation, the oligarchs are dominating the masses via instruments of power and power relations that mock the discourse of democracy and revolution. Fanon continues: "Thus, on the level of the whole colonized society, we always discover this resistance to qualify opposition to the colonialist, for it so happens that every qualification is perceived by the occupier as an invitation to perpetuate the oppression, as a confession of congenital impotence." (Fanon 1965 pg. 122). In the neo-colonial condition this persists, even though we are all free in a free nation, because the domination/hegemony exercised by the oligarchs and the political elite is patterned after the colonial model of domination by dint of conquest. In the neo-colonial condition there can be no qualification of opposition as it sends messages of weakness which intensifies the repression and barbarity and since we are reputedly free people in a free nation, our opposition adopts the mode of the expression of extremism. Extremist violence against races, ethnic groups, classes, individuals all defined as enemies is then the order of the day. Opposition as defined and enabled by the constitution of the free nation is viewed by the oligarchs and their political elite as weakness, as betrayal of the Revolution and a plausible threat to the vanguard of the Revolution. As under colonial domination, all opposition is unconstitutional and extremist and the order of engagement in a free Algeria remains as that of the colonizer, hence neo-colonial in spite of the Algerian Revolution, the absolute unleashed on French colonial domination. Such is the example of Algeria from the Revolution to the present. Fanon continues: "The fact is that the colonization, having been built on military conquest and the police system, sought a justification for its existence and the legitimization of its persistence in its works." (Fanon 1965 pg. 122). The ruling politicians and the oligarchs they serve inherit the colonial state with its military and police intact, cast in the mold of instruments of colonial domination. These instruments of colonial power are embraced and redirected to ensure the hegemony of the ruling politicians and the oligarchy they serve. These two colonial repressive instruments of the masses are never dismantled, reformulated and newly visioned as instruments in the service of the masses towards recognition of and respect for the power of the masses. The military and police inherited from the colonial order remain charged with suppressing the power of the masses and ensuring the hegemony of a new local oligarchy. In Algeria, the revolutionary elite ensured that they dominated the revolutionary military before the defeat of the colonizer. With victory the military became the tool of the revolutionary elite to ensure the hegemony of the revolutionary oligarchy. Faced with electoral defeat at the hands of the Islamic alternative in the 1990s, the instrument of the military wielded in the interest of the oligarchy staged the coup that ended this threat and invited Islamic Extremism to now become a player on the battlefields of Algeria, thereby justifying the coup that destroyed the power of the masses once and for all. Resorting to repression in the event of threats to the hegemony of the oligarchy and the politicians indicates that the process of legitimization of the regime has not assured hegemony by consent and/or acquiescence of the masses. The process of legitimization in the neo-colonial condition involves manipulating the symbols of the free nation, formulated by the oligarchs for mass consumption, combined with and buttressed with patronage, political and other forms. The colonial State form is retained as it is vitally necessary to repress, dispense patronage, tax the population, borrow and spend. The colonial State form is then multifaceted as it enables dispensing patronage, plunder necessary to amass personal and family wealth and to repress the masses and non-compliant individuals and groups. The colonial State form is never destroyed and a State form rooted in the power of the masses is never constructed for it is inconvenient to the realization of the hegemony of a native oligarchy to allow this process to be undertaken. This neo-colonial/colonial State hybrid was established to serve the strategy of the hegemony of an oligarchy over the post-colonial free society, which meant that the intent of the Revolution in Algeria was to replace the white colonizer with a native oligarchy. The masses then never exerted their hegemony over the Revolution, hence were at the mercy of the Revolutionary elite with victory. Which indicates that a Revolution against colonial domination will assault the colonial psycho-existential complex and its impact on the colonized, but in no way does it prepare the masses to deal with the power relations of the neo-colonial condition as it leaves the masses open to the ravages of the psycho-existential complex formulated and unleashed by the revolutionary elite to ensure the servility of the masses. The psycho-existential complex unleashed by the revolutionary elite exhibits potency that the colonial instrument only dreamt about, hence the importance of neo-colonial oligarchs to sustainable white, North Atlantic hegemony over the post-colonial world. Fanon continues on the colonial condition as follows: "It is not possible for the colonized society and the colonizing society to agree to pay tribute, at the same time and in the same place, to a single value." (Fanon 1965 pg. 126). This was the inherent operational problem of white colonial domination over non-white peoples seeking to extend colonial domination in the aftermath of the second world war. This operational problematic did not exist in the case of the neo-colonial condition where a local, native oligarchy was now exerting hegemony over the masses making it the obvious operational choice. But narrow nationalist, white supremacist discourse could not envisage the collapse of empire and the need to change the power relation between the white North Atlantic and the new native hegemonic oligarchies. In the post second world war context of decolonization, the US led the way in pioneering the new terms of endearment under US hegemony.

Fanon now analyses the context of colonial and Revolutionary medical care in Algeria as follows: "It is now necessary to enter into the tragic labyrinth of the general reactions of Algerian society with respect to the problem of the fight against illness, conceived as an aspect of the French presence. We shall then see in the course of the fight for liberation the crystallization of the new attitude adopted by the Algerian people in respect to medical techniques." (Fanon 1965 pg. 126). The Algerian masses did not trust the medical infrastructure of the colonizer viewing it with suspicion as an instrument of domination and Algerian genocide. This fear of the medical infrastructure of the colonizer effectively politicized colonial medicine where the fact of illness was subject to the fear of the colonizer and the terms of engagement defined by the Algerian, governing contact with the medical infrastructure of the colonizer. The revolutionary medical infrastructure liberated the Algerian from the terms of engagement adopted, thereby enabling the acceptance of medical intervention to mitigate illness. But the salient issue is what type of medicine is revolutionary medicine, for if it's western medicine with a revolutionary veneer there is no patient power just the hegemony of medical discourse, another instrument of the power wielded by the revolutionary oligarchy. Fanon states: "The colonial situation standardizes relations, for it dichotomizes the colonial society in a marked way." (Fanon 1965 pg. 126). The neo-colonial condition dichotomizes the social order in a much more fundamental manner than the colonial order as the distinction between colonizer and colonized was readily apparent with skin color, physical characteristics. Colonial power is white, white is might and always right. The neo-colonial oligarchy has to relentlessly strive to distinguish itself from the masses, hence the use of all differences real, imagined and constituted to distinguish themselves from the masses and to dichotomize the masses into hostile groups. That is why in the neo-colonial condition difference that distinguishes the oligarchy from the masses is always ostentatiously displayed publicly, to the extent of being hedonistic. The colonizer need not be ostentatious as she/he was secure in the genetic dichotomy of the skin. Fanon points out that the very basis of medical truth between the colonizer and colonized was impossible given colonial domination as follows: "The truth objectively expressed is constantly vitiated by the lie of the colonial situation." (Fanon 1965 pg. 128). Under the neo-colonial condition the lie persists but it is much more potent, aggressive and organic as the colonizer is absent but the hegemony of the oligarchy ensures that all instruments of power that constituted the colonizer's lie are deployed, utilized and evolved to a state of potency, where non-white genocide unleashed by non-white actors is now on the agenda of the oligarchy. In Algeria the lie was never dismantled, simply embraced, reformulated and unleashed by the revolutionary elite in its quest for hegemony as an oligarchy. Fanon continues: "Colonial domination, as we have seen, gives rise to and continues to dictate a whole complex of resentful behavior and of refusal on the part of the colonized." (Fanon 1965 pg. 130). Under the neo-colonial condition domination continues, it's heightened and intensified as it drives the neo-colonial psycho-existential complex in the bid of the hegemonic oligarchy to have the masses problematise themselves, towards having the instruments of power render them docile. The masses then alienate themselves from the daily operations of the State only where it is absolutely necessary for their daily survival, as it is a hostile space that alienates and potently illustrates their powerlessness in their interaction with the State machinery. The neo-colonial oligarchy embraces the colonial state form, expands its expanse and power over the daily life of the masses, whilst ensuring that the masses have no power over the State. The State becomes the expression of the power over the masses of the hegemonic oligarchy. Post-revolutionary Algeria is a potent example of this neo-colonial process. Fanon states: "Colonialism obviously throws all the elements of native society into confusion. The dominant group arrives with its values and imposes them with such violence that the very life of the colonized can manifest itself only defensively, in a more or less clandestine way. Under these conditions, colonial domination distorts the very relations that the colonized maintain with their own culture." (Fanon 1965 pg. 130). Colonial domination assaults native society constituting native culture that is constantly second guessing itself and its worldview. The assaulted native culture simply is not at peace with itself as it does not affirm itself and it is under constant pressure to have the colonizer affirm it. The neo-colonial oligarchy embraces this wounded culture, heightens its dependency to the extent where it must now be affirmed by the hegemonic oligarchy. Neo-colonial politics goes into the business of formulating and propagandizing cultural values that were supposedly anti-colonial, but formulated by their discursive agents for the masses. This discourse of acceptable culture formulated by the oligarchs, heightens the cultural confusion inherited from the colonial era, in its quest to divide the masses against itself where race/ethnic war is unleashed. The hegemonic oligarchy does not embrace nor publicly indicate their embrace of the neo-colonial culture they prescribe for the masses. What they do embrace is the globalized culture of the colonizer, which in the case of Algeria frames the embrace of the alternate to that of the revolutionary elite that appeared in the 1990s. Whilst the evolution of the power relation in Algeria from the 1990s to the present reveals the inability of the Algerian to emancipate themselves from the limitations imposed by this wounded culture peddled from colonization to the neo-colonial condition, as both the masses and the hegemonic oligarchy are trapped in a netherworld where the formulation of emancipatory action is proscribed, even prohibited by a wounded national culture. Fanon ends this train of thought as follows: "Once again the colonial world reveals itself to be complex and extremely diverse in structure. There is always an opposition of exclusive worlds, a contradictory interaction of different techniques, a vehement confrontation of values." (Fanon 1965 pg. 131). The neo-colonial world trapped in the neo-colonial condition and post-revolution Algeria retain these characteristics, have heightened them, made them more complex, more combative and added specific developments of the free nation under the power of a hegemonic oligarchy and an external hegemon of the North Atlantic. The basis of this neo-colonial reality is the expansion and hardening of exclusion, where exclusive worlds now face each other premised on graphic scenes of inequality versus privilege/entitlement, power and powerlessness. Out of this opposition of exclusive worlds the culture of nihilism inherited from colonial domination has evolved into the nihilism of the criminal insurgency, which

presents the potent challenge at present to the 21st century neo-colonial condition.

Fanon now deals with the colonized native who is a doctor and her/his interaction with the colonized. Fanon states: "There is a manifest ambivalence of the colonized group with respect to any member who acquires a technique or the manners of the colonizer." "The native doctor is a Europeanized, Westernized doctor, and in certain circumstances he is considered as being no longer part of the dominated society. He is tacitly rejected into the camp of the oppressors, into the opposing camp." "The native doctor feels himself psychologically compelled to demonstrate firmly his new admission to a rational universe." "The native doctor, because of the operation of the complex psychological laws that govern colonial society, frequently finds himself in a difficult position." (Fanon 1965 pgs. 131-132). The native doctor is alienated from the masses as she/he is alienated from their non-white selves, but committed to western medical discourse they can only be an instrument of power of the colonizer. But the native doctor finds her/his calling and comes into their own with the Revolution and the neo-colonial condition that follows given the embrace of western discourse and its attendant worldview by the hegemonic oligarchy. The native doctor becomes the symbol of the potency of the neo-colonial state of existence, where she/ he is enveloped by western discourse yet free, creative and wielding power. The native doctor is then the symbol of modernity erasing the backwardness of the former colony unleashing western progress under the domination of the hegemonic oligarchy. The native doctor sums up the hegemony of western discourse over the entire structure of ideational formulation under the neo-colonial condition, which constitutes the colonization of the free nation at the level of the idea by the west. This structure of ideas is passive, a recipient of unquestioned discourse from the west which effectively renders the neo-colonial order brain dead, incapable of the necessary action to ensure a sustainable social order rooted in innovation and creativity. This is an existential condition worse than that of colonial domination for there is no hope, hopelessness and nihilism abound for that is the fruit of colonization at the level of the idea. The native doctor is then a willing participant and active supporter of the strategy of the hegemonic oligarchy, choosing personally not to be an agent of healing, but of exploitation and repression for personal gain and wealth accumulation by draining the resources of the masses through their mystique as gods of healing, given the inherent superiority of all things white and western. This agenda is replicated through all expertise rooted in western discourse, where they are in fact the pirates of the neo-colonial condition preying on the masses.

Fanon now deals with the white doctor and the Algerian Revolution by insisting that she/he is a settler, an instrument of power of colonial domination. Fanon states: "Generally speaking, the colonizing doctor adopts the attitude of his group toward the struggle of the Algerian people." "Whether the land has come to him from his family, or he has bought it himself, the doctor is a settler." (Fanon 1965 pg. 133). The white doctor is a settler, thereby having a stake in the colonial enterprise and a personal interest in defeating the Algerian revolution. The white colonizer has an economic, personal and race interest in maintaining white supremacy over Algeria. This multi-functionality of the white colonizer doctor illustrates the order and nature of the colonial social order as follows: "Colonial society is a mobile society, poorly structured, and the European, even when he is a technician, always assumes a certain degree of polyvalence." (Fanon 1965 pg. 133). The white settler doctor is situated in a colonial social order as an operational instrument of colonial power, with presence and operational activity in a number of power relations spanning multiple instruments of power, thereby colonial power is polyvalent as the instruments of power are polyvalent. The settler doctor is settler, medical technician and torturer simultaneously. Power is polyvalent in the colonial social order because it is a mobile social order caused by its poor structure, as it is divided simply on a Manichean duality: white, colonizer/non-white, colonized. This simplistic structuring then demands that power be served by mobile, multitasking human actors of both white and non-white segments, one to dominate, the other to be dominated. Under the social order of post-revolution Algeria the hegemonic oligarchy replicated the colonial social order with a simplistic division of hegemonic revolutionary elite and the masses, the dominator and the dominated, where both the dominator and the dominated must be mobile and polyvalent. In the case of the masses they are required to be mobile simply for the exercise of daily survival, given the inequality that constitutes the deprivation that afflicts them when compared to the hegemonic oligarchy. The demands of being polyvalent to survive on a daily basis, or the hustle, detracts from being tactically polyvalent in the political arena, necessary to exerting mass power on the oligarchy. This is the instrument of power unleashed and wielded by the hegemonic oligarchy, the ever potent weapon of deprivation. The oligarchs are called upon to be mobile and polyvalent vitally necessary to sustainable domination and wealth accumulation, which indicates that the colonial project continues in the 21st century, even though the white settler colonizer has been expelled. Fanon continues: "The European individual in Algeria does not take his place in a structured and relatively stable society. The colonialist society is in perpetual movement. Every settler invents a new society, sets up or sketches new structures. The differences between craftsmen, civil servants, workers, and professionals are poorly defined. Every doctor has his vineyards and the lawyer busies himself with his rice fields as passionately as any settler. The doctor is not socially defined by the exercise of his profession alone. He is likewise the owner of mills, wine cellars, or orange groves," "In Algeria we must not be surprised to find that doctors and professors are leaders of colonialist movements." (Fanon 1965 pg. 134). The white settler colonizer has to be polyvalent to maximize the extraction of wealth from the colony, to maximize the collection of personal wealth and to ensure the sustainability of the colonial enterprise premised on the hegemony of a small, oligarchy of a minority race of foreigners. The defeat of the colonizer enables the replacement of the white oligarchy with the native oligarchy, intent on replicating the model of the rapacious white colonial oligarchy. The members of this native oligarchy are not defined by their profession, but by their polyvalence exhibited through the instruments of power formulated and unleashed to exploit the wealth of Algeria and wield sustainable power over the masses to their personal benefit. Every single member of this Algerian oligarchy wields power, amasses personal wealth, acts as agents of North Atlantic interests that exploit Algerian wealth and are instruments of power in the domination of the masses. The colonial order of the settler has evolved to suit the strategic terrain, but was never dismantled as those wielding revolutionary power emulated the settler, indicating that they surrendered to white supremacy at the level of the idea. Fanon continues: "On the strictly technical level, the European doctor actively collaborates with the colonial forces in their most frightful and most degrading practices." "In the European medical corps in Algeria, and especially in the military health corps, such things are common. Professional morality, medical ethics, self-respect and respect for others, have given to the most uncivilized, the most degrading, the most perverse kind of behavior." (Fanon 1965 pgs. 137-138). In the quest to maintain the hegemony of the white colonial oligarchy, all white action is driven by the strategy to defeat any form of native resistance by any means necessary. A pragmatic where morality, ethics and principles are weaponized in the quest to defeat the native insurgency by disarming the insurgents at the level of the idea. In post-revolution Algeria the revolutionary oligarchy adopts the same strategy, where it betrays the revolutionary discourse articulated during the Revolution at the personal level, whilst insisting that the masses remain bound by this revolutionary discourse binding them to the revolutionary oligarchy. Revolutionary principles do not apply to them and they are above revolutionary policing, whilst the masses are obligated to, need to be policed by the revolutionary oligarchy and are counter revolutionary when they question the discourse of the revolution articulated by the hegemonic oligarchy. The revolution begins and ends with the oligarchy, not the masses illustrating the domination of an oligarchy cast in the mold of the white colonizer, not an anti-colonial revolution. The Revolutionary elite was then never organic to the masses but to the white colonizer, seeking simply to replace the white colonizer with themselves continuing the exploitation of the masses and Algeria.

In the final section of this chapter Fanon deals with white science, especially medicine, weaponized against the Revolution, where whites in Algeria policed the blockade established to prevent access by Algerians to medical supplies in an attempt to break the back of the insurgency. Fanon states: "The European would return, loaded down with medicines, relaxed, innocent. Such experiences have not made it easy for the Algerians to keep a balanced judgment towards members of the European minority. Science depoliticized, science in the service of man, is often non-existent in the colonies." (Fanon 1965 pg. 140). The white discourse of science is never depoliticized as it is an instrument of power in the North Atlantic. When deployed in the power relations of white colonial domination of non-whites it's deployed to serve white supremacy in the context of colonial domination. Revolutionary science must then be depoliticized and in the service of the masses, but Revolutionary Algeria never formulated and unleashed its discourse of Revolutionary science, choosing instead to embrace the white discourse of a science thereby ensuring its hegemony at the level of the idea during the Revolution and post-revolution Algeria. Revolutionary Algeria was then rooted in a discourse of science that ensured and illustrated its neo-colonial dependence on the North Atlantic at the level of the idea. As a result of this neo-colonisation at the level of the idea, the discursive apparatus of Revolutionary and post-revolution Algeria were all clones of a North Atlantic discursive apparatus, which meant that the discursive production of Revolutionary and especially post-revolution Algeria were in keeping with white, North Atlantic models. The white person and power of the colonizer was expelled and replaced by the white expert in all branches of the white, North Atlantic knowledge production apparatus of post-revolution Algeria. The hegemonic oligarchy insists on whitening Algeria from the level of the idea, for that is the level of comfort with themselves they desire. You can then remove the physical presence of the white, colonial dominator through violence with your embrace of white discourse and knowledge immune from assault from the process of removing the immediate colonizer. With victory the potency and power of the white idea that you define yourself by and view the world with is exerted and exhibited as power wielded enhances its power of seduction, especially geopolitical power.

The embrace of the white discourse of science in the post-colonial context is then a potent indicator of the continued enslavement of the former colonized, supposedly in a context of decolonization at the level of the idea. The Algerian revolution was then betrayed by a revolutionary elite steeped in white scientific discourse, intent on replicating the colonial model with a native, non-white elite now exerting hegemony over the native masses, and to ensure the success of this narrow, personal agenda this revolutionary elite surrendered to the hegemony of the white North Atlantic world at the level of the idea, which was expressed via the various actions employed by this elite.

Chapter 5
Algeria's Hegemonic White Minority

In the final chapter of Fanon's work he analyses the discourse of the white minority of Algeria on the Algerian Revolution and the means to ensure its defeat. Fanon insists that this hegemonic race minority is not monolithic as it consists of factions with contradictory discourses. One such faction views the Algerian Revolution in apocalyptic terms as the non-white natives are threatening the very sustainable existence of Algeria made in the image and likeness of white hegemony. This is the white supremacist discourse of conquest and white race entitlement which demands that the white race defend its entitlement to the point of unleashing genocide. Fanon states: "The traditionalists of colonization have long ago been outdistanced. This is because the new kingpins of the colonization see the future in apocalyptic terms. Some of Algeria's European intellectuals, because they have links with the colonial power, have often contributed to giving the Algerian war its hallucinatory character. We have seen doctors assigned full time to the dispensaries of the judicial police, and we know that philosophers and priests in the relocation or internment centers, assume the mission of brain-washing, of probing souls, of making the Algerian man unrecognizable." (Fanon 1965 pgs. 147-148). White solidarity has galvanized white apocalyptic action against the Algerian in an attempt to break the back of the insurgency. The white response to the native insurgency has then a hallucinatory character, even a lunatic tinge to it as they are acting on the position that native insurgency will only end with white genocide, hence the necessity of first unleashing native genocide. This position is rooted in the belief that the whites have the means and the impunity to effect such native genocide as they expect white solidarity will result in a compliant France launching this native genocide, with a level of efficiency, with the desired kill rate outstripping that presently of the outcome of France's anti-insurgency efforts in Algeria. The discourse of white supremacy, as it always does when faced by a grave non-white threat, was now in Algeria acting on the expectation that France will comply with their demand for the Final Solution. In the 21st century the North Atlantic is now actively in search of apocalyptic solutions to the Chinese threat. For the interim, until the native genocide is unleashed and attained, the task at hand for white solidarity was breaking the back of the insurgency by erasing the Algerian through the application of measured, deliberate, debilitating violence mixed with violent cleansing of specific Algerians, which proved to be the product of a worldview driven by white hallucinations.

Fanon now deals with the political movements of France, especially those who insist that they are democrats at heart and of the white left and their position on the Algerian Revolution. Fanon states: "France, as an imperialist country, has great racist potentialities, as we have seen more clearly in the past two years, but among Frenchmen there are reflexes that operate spontaneously. This accounts for the relative freedom left to opponents-less and less, however, because, France is beginning to be colonized by the Algerian activists-and this accounts for the outbursts of public indignation that greets every revelation that reaches France regarding the torture practiced in Algeria." (Fanon 1965 pg. 150). The call to white solidarity in France with the settlers of Algeria finds traction in a white supremacist France and this is heightened by the deliberate actions of the Algerian settler lobby to persuade the electorate of France that their final solution for Algeria is acceptable, feasible and indeed the only recourse. What has then to be erased is the dichotomy between the embrace of white colonial supremacy and the myth of France being a modern, civilized, white democracy of exemplary commitment to human rights and the rights of man. For the embrace of this myth arouses public uneasiness with the strategy devised and applied to break the back of the insurgency in Algeria. In the 21st century the world hegemon, the USA, has no such problem when destroying threats to white supremacy. In this scenario, those who insist that they embrace the rights of man and democracy and are on the left of North Atlantic politics are part of the drive to shore up white world hegemony through the world dominance of the USA. Fanon is apologetic for the failure of the left to impact the politics of France countering the influence of French white supremacist colonial discourse as he insists that they are playing the role of a stumbling block which is contributing to eventual victory. Fanon states: "Because of their own contradictions and because of the power and the radicalism of the reactionary parties, the forces of the Left in France have up to the present time been unable to impose negotiation. But undeniably they are forcing the extremists to unmask themselves, and hence progressively to adopt the position that will precipitate their defeat." (Fanon 1964 pg. 150). Fanon's natural discursive allies in French politics are yet to impact French politics in any manner that places on the political agenda an alternate French strategy. For Fanon that is negotiation, and for Fanon it is desirable, but this reveals Fanon's mindset for negotiation with France, including Fanon's Left, is the means to allow the Left to sell the Algerian Revolution down the river with the revolutionary elite in tow. For in actual negotiation the white supremacist agenda for Algeria of the French Left will be revealed giving the revolutionary elite the choice of no choice. Take it or leave it and we return to the barbarity of the Right. This is the quintessential good cop/ bad cop play of the white supremacist on non-white people faced with the threat of genocide unleashed on us. Fanon now states that in Algeria there are no white democrats and leftists. Fanon states: "In Algeria the forces of the left do not exist. It is unthinkable for European democrats really to militate in Algeria outside the Algerian Communist Party." "Algeria's European democrats have from the beginning lived in a more or less clandestine state. Drowned in the European mass, they live in a world of values that their principles reject and condemn. The European democrat is on the defensive. He has contacts with Algerians but in secrecy. In the European colony he is referred to as the 'Arab.'" (Fanon 1965 pgs. 150-151). The white democrat and leftist is an endangered species in white settler Algeria, for they present a threat to sustainable white hegemony over Algeria; for white settler supremacy is extremism personified as no discourse that views the non-white as a human is tolerable, much less acceptable. White settler supremacy then insists that you cannot negotiate with animals, which means that the only solution to the Algerian insurgency is genocide and white morals and values only apply to white people, not non-white people in subjection to white people. The grave threat perceived, posed by China in the 21st century to white USA's world hegemony, demands genocide to mitigate this threat once and for all. As the threat posed grows intense and extreme, white genocide will now rise to the apex of the perceptual pyramid justifying Chinese genocide as a defensive measure, a pre-emptory strike in the preservation of white USA's world hegemony.

Fanon now deals with the position of the Jews of Algeria on the Revolution. Fanon recognizes the Jewish traders as being supportive of French colonial domination as they are the recipients of privilege under colonial apartheid, which shields them from non-Jewish native competition. This colonial apartheid created the second group of privileged Jews of Algeria, the civil servants, being the only locals recruited to the colonial civil service, to the detriment of the non-Jewish natives, and hence supportive of colonial domination. The third and largest group of Jews comprise those with the least contact with the colonial order, are rooted in native culture with its Jewish definition and actively support the revolution. The Jews of Algeria illustrate the instrument of power wielded by colonial domination towards dividing the masses on the basis of race and ethnicity as defined by white supremacist discourse. The colonized are seduced to accept concepts of race and ethnic difference that were alien to their cultures, which are activated by deliberate action of the colonizer through the colonial apartheid system, thereby constituting the self-fulfilling prophecy. In the neo-colonial condition this instrument of power continues to be wielded by the oligarchs unleashing genocide as a political weapon of social control. In post-revolutionary Algeria, the oligarchy embraced and breathed new life into this colonial instrument of power towards dividing the masses in a bid to avert any threats arising from mass action. Fanon describes the dynamics of self-hate of those Jews who are active agents of the colonial war against the masses. Fanon states: "Finally, colonial Algeria being an eminently racist country, the different mechanisms of racist psychology are to be found there. Thus the Jews, despised and excluded by the Europeans, is quite happy on certain occasions to identify himself with those who humiliate him to humiliate the Algerian in turn." (Fanon 1965 pg. 154). The Algerian Jew is the proxy of colonial apartheid as he is taught that he is superior to the Arab, the Muslim, the Amazighs, but grossly inferior to the white colonizer to whom he must be ever thankful for affording such privilege. This Jew, afflicted with hallucinatory whiteness, must relentlessly prove his worth to the white master race by shitting on his race inferiors, but no matter what he does he can never be white. Self-hate drives him to these acts in the service of hegemonic white supremacist discourse as he must feel superior in dumping on his inferiors as designated by the discourse of white supremacy, even though he is one such inferior to the master race. Likewise, the Arab must do the same, repeat the same process with the same dynamic, both ensuring the hegemony of white supremacy. Both Jew and Arab are in the 21st century summed up in the geo-political expressions: Israel and the Palestinians, where two non-white races burdened with hallucinatory whiteness pour out white supremacist hate on each other jostling for the affirmation of the master race with a history of genocide unleashed on both non-white races.

Fanon ends this chapter by presenting the words of a white male born in Algeria who considers himself an Algerian in support of the Algerian Revolution. Fanon states: "French colonialism refuses to admit that a genuine European can really fight side by side with the Algerian people." (Fanon 1965 pg. 160). This then is the testimony of a white male that falsifies the white supremacist position of French colonial discourse and in turn gives us insight into what Fanon considers a "genuine European." The testimony states: "The absence of curiosity with regards to our country's burning problems had its origin, it must be recognized, in the unconscious race prejudice we all bore within us having been inoculated by twenty years of colonial life. Being of the Left, we had, to be sure, surmounted the aggressive colonial racism, but we had by no means rid ourselves of paternalism. Not the least of the shocks that we experienced was the realization that we were still racist in attitude." (Fanon 1965 pg. 164). The discourse of the Left of the Enlightenment naturally deconstructed the rabid racism of French colonial aggression, but it failed to purge white supremacy expressed as the inherent superiority of the white race. The white, leftist male can never grasp that he has never purged himself of white supremacy, as his leftist worldview is rooted in the discourse of white supremacy, enabling him to disparage an instrument of white supremacy whilst simultaneously holding on to its fundamental tenets. He is then a potent example of the white male leftist of his day, who is a genuine European, but his worldview flows with that of the revolutionary elite of Algeria. The testimony continues as follows: "Race prejudice had crystallized under the pressure of events, and it was impossible to get people to think dispassionately," "What Algeria's Frenchmen were most worried about, in fact, was whether or not they would be able to remain in Algeria. Having to leave-whether for France, Canada or Brazil (as some were contemplating)-meant exile." (Fanon 1965 pgs. 167-168). You insist Algeria is yours by dint of conquest, but you are a hegemonic minority through the unleashing of violence on the non-white majority. Now that this violence has failed to ensure white hegemony you can only envisage genocide, for it is preferable to exile from what is yours by dint of conquest. This was a colony, and quite expendable, but the reaction is not the same when the white heartland is gravely threatened by a non-white threat. Then the only feasible response is the Final Solution. The testimony now comes to the crux of the matter for a genuine European is as follows: "Independence, yes, I agreed wholeheartedly. But what independence? Were we going to fight to build a theocratic, feudal, Moslem state that frowned on foreigners? Who could claim that we had a place in such an Algeria?" (Fanon 1965 pg. 168). The genuine European agrees that Algeria must be independent from France, but the crux of the matter is what constitutes the post-revolution Algeria for Algeria is unwelcoming to white people if it is a Muslim state. The Muslim state is theocratic, hence undemocratic, backward and incapable of progress for it is feudal, hence unwelcoming to genuine Europeans. What is then needed is the neo-colonial condition with its dependence on white hegemony, thereby creating an Algeria which is welcoming to genuine Europeans as the author of the testimonial. The Revolutionary elite then gave this genuine European the assurance he desired as the oligarchs of the North Atlantic got what was desired, thereby destroying the Revolution. Genuine Europeans of whatever political persuasion desire the neo-colonial condition, if not they are whites who have committed race suicide.

Fanon ends the book with his Conclusions where he states: "This community in action, renovated and free of any psychological, emotional or legal subjection, is prepared today to assume modern and democratic responsibilities of exceptional moment." (Fanon 1965 pg. 179). The act of engaging with the colonizer in battle has removed the impediments imposed by colonial domination that prohibited a post-colonial Algeria from becoming a modern

democratic nation of rare renown. Since Algeria in the 21st century is in no way a modern democracy of rare renown, then the problem has to be found in the way revolutionary discourse defined modernity and democracy, thereby deliberately hobbling the process of dynamic change. Or the revolutionary act of expelling the colonizer and the purging of the impediments imposed on Algerians by colonial domination cannot and does not preclude the development and evolution of power relations that are common to the neo-colonial condition in former colonial states granted independence as a gift from the colonizer. Revolution in essence then cannot prevent a revolutionary elite from hijacking the revolution to the detriment of the masses, or worse yet the revolutionary discourse formulated and dispersed by the revolutionary elite effectively enables their evolution into a revolutionary oligarchy with victory over the colonizer. This power grab is enabled by revolutionary discourse utilized to defeat the colonizer, whilst it renders the masses powerless. The basis of this power grab by the revolutionary elite is the white secular discourse of revolution embraced by Fanon and the revolutionary elite rooted in the Enlightenment and white supremacist discourse of the North Atlantic. Hence the replication of the neo-colonial condition in the aftermath of a revolution in Algeria, thereby falsifying Fanon's position. Fanon continues: "The Revolution in depth, the true one, precisely because it changes man and renews society, has reached an advanced stage. The oxygen which creates and shapes a new humanity-this too, is the Algerian Revolution." (Fanon 1965 pg. 181). The revolution removed a colonizer, but failed to create a new human in Algeria as the revolutionary oligarchy has shown its willingness to venture into barbarity against the masses last seen under colonial domination. What binds the revolutionary oligarchy to the white colonizer oligarchy is the position that Algeria is theirs won by conquest, and they both will defend their hegemony by any barbarous means necessary. The commonality then is power and power relations where under a revolution the power relations resemble colonial power relations, not revolutionary power relations with the masses wielding power. Fanon states: "We have indicated that strictly on the level of the individual and his tremendous dynamism a revolution-fundamental, irreversible, ever more far-reaching has occurred." (Fanon 1965 pg. 180). This revolution-fundamental at the level of the individual was under the hegemony of the revolutionary elite towards the defeat of the colonizer, but with victory the revolution-fundamental now lacked a new target as the revolutionary elite began the process of turning the revolution-fundamental against itself dividing the masses into warring factions, which enabled the evolution of the elite into an oligarchy in command of the social order. The revolutionary elite accomplished their task by applying the methodology of the white French colonizer to the post-colonial Algeria in the formulation of the State/social order. Fanon describes the French methodology as follows: "Every manifestation of the French presence expressed a continuous rooting in time and in the Algerian future, and could always be read as a token of an indefinite oppression. It was the size of the French settlement, the rapacity of the settlers and their racist philosophy that required of every French expression in Algeria a maximum of solidity and of weight. Likewise, it was the robustness and vehemence of French achievements that maintained and reinforced the oppressive category of colonialism." (Fanon 1965 pg. 180). A most potent description of the nature of the hegemony of the revolutionary oligarchy in the 21st century in Algeria where this oligarchy insists that it is the revolution and without it there would be no revolution, hence Algeria is theirs by dint of conquest from the French, they are entitled to Algeria. Fanon did not live to behold the evolution of his beloved Revolution and his belief in the Revolution as absolute never wavered until his death. But his discourse provides instruments by which to strip bare the nakedness of the Algerian revolution at present, which ultimately raises the issue of power and power relations and the consummate failure of a paradigm of revolution against white supremacist domination borrowed from the Enlightenment and its white supremacist discourse. Fanon was then walking the minefield of a discourse and its attendant worldview that he exposed for its white supremacist worldview, whilst holding dear to a discourse of revolution as absolute that was the product of the said discourse. Fanon was than afflicted with the ambivalence of those seeking escape from white discourse, yet simultaneously seeking alternatives amongst white discourse. The ambivalence that destroys the soul arising from the failure to journey through alternate, non-white discourses of the world.

Chapter 6
Toward the African Revolution

In "Toward the African Revolution" Fanon's articles on the Algerian Revolution were published posthumously. What follows is a deconstruction of specific articles chosen from those published.

The Strategy for Sustainable French Colonial Domination of Algeria

Published in El Moudjahid, No. 10, September 1957

Fanon in this article is analyzing the strategy unleashed by France in specific stages to defeat the Algerian Revolution from 1954 to the time of writing. Fanon states: "not enough has been said of the stereotypes of means used by the parent countries to cling to their colonies. The Franco-Algerian war, because of its size and intensity, enables us to see in close-up, by the very reason of her successive failures, the attempts made by France to maintain her domination." (Fanon 1967 pg. 57). The discourse of the white man's burden is relentlessly used to justify colonial conquest and domination and makes its contribution to formulating the discourse of independence as a 'gift' from the master race, to an inferior race made deserving of independence by colonial conquest and domination. But the stereotypical slew of measures unleashed to break the back of an anti-colonial movement in the colonies, that repeatedly fails to do so, is never part of the discourse of colonial domination and independence as a gift. In this article Fanon is presenting such an analysis in terms of the Franco-Algerian war.

The first tactic/operation

Fanon states: "The first tactic of the colonial countries consist of basing themselves on official collaborators and feudal elements." "In 1954 and the first months of 1955 France proceeded to make a census of its faithful and loyal servants and to mobilize them." (Fanon 1967 pg. 57). The first tactic unleashed with its consequent operation of the French in the war against the Algerian revolution was to mobilize its Algerian collaborators for the assault on the revolution. This was then essentially a strategy to divide the non-white population through warring factions with the hope and intent of overwhelming the revolution as a besieged minority. The Algerian must then police the Algerian to the benefit of massa and sustainable colonial domination. Fanon states: "The fact is that the revolutionary commitment proved to be more and more total and the collaborators became aware of the gigantic awakening of a people in arms." (Fanon 1967 pg. 58). The collaborators got the message that they were in fact the besieged minority as the masses were now signaling their rejection of the yoke of French colonial domination. But the colonizers were in denial as they refused to accept the reality of the scale and expanse of the rejection by the masses of their domination by the white colonizer. This denial can only then formulate the Final Solution.

The second tactic/operation

The French finally accepted the need for a second stage when they saw their longest serving collaborators switching sides, refusing to serve them any further and most painfully when the non-white colonial elite they created to serve them now expressed open hostility to the white colonizer. The realization of a crisis sparked the formulation and unleashing of the second tactic/operation which defined the cause of the revolution as economic deprivation, poverty which will be addressed vigorously by a colonial intervention into the economic reality of the colonized masses. The Algerian in revolt can then be bought with a mess of pottage. Fanon states: "Essentially this amounted to cutting of the presumably 'sound' population from the revolutionary movement. Incapable of apprehending the real significance of the battle for liberation, France in a first stage recognized the existence of a problem which it declared to be economic and social." "This treatment of a demand for national liberation as if it were a peasant uprising, or a manifestation of social discontent, resulted from a double confusion: the idea that there is no Algerian national consciousness on the one hand, and on the other, the conviction that the promises of the improvement of the living standard of the population would suffice to bring back order and peace." (Fanon 1967 pg. 58). The colonizer cannot accept and act on the reality that colonization was the problem, hence the war of liberation. The problem must then be conceptualized as having an economic basis which could foster a successful colonizer intervention. The strategy called for a number of interventions that would raise the standard of living of the poorest in Algeria, thereby inoculating them from mobilization by the revolutionary forces. The core concept of the resistance of the colonizer to break the back of the revolution was mobilizing the necessary volume of Algerians complicit with colonization to defend the colonizer against the revolution. This was conceptualized as a war fought by Algerians against Algerians for the benefit of the white, colonial hegemonic oligarchy. Very early after the launch of the war for liberation in 1954 it became apparent that this strategy had failed miserably, necessitating the final solution. The brutal war unleashed by the colonizer on Algerians indicated the failure of the colonial strategy which heightened the brutality in response to every setback and defeat. There was then need for a second stage under the second tactic/operation. In this second stage the colonizer played the card of race and ethnic division amongst the minorities of Algeria towards heightening race divisions, thereby cutting away these minorities from the revolutionary forces. The attempt was to identify the minorities with the colonizer with the intent of fomenting a race war which will engulf and quench the drive for liberation by the masses. Fanon states: "In the second stage, and with a rare duplicity, the French administration organised the Mozabite operation, the Kabyle operation, the Jewish operation, the *harka* operation." "These operations were characterized by the exploitation of a certain number of local hostilities created by colonialism, the maintenance and the provoked intensification of cultural differences transformed into feuds between clans or, in some cases, between 'races.'" (Fanon 1967 pg. 59). The colonizer targeted the minorities of Algeria: non-Arab, non-Muslim and both, where under colonial domination differences were perpetuated to differentiate these minorities from the masses to perpetuate the conviction that they were under attack and marked for elimination by the revolution. The method used were false flag attacks/harka blamed on the revolutionary forces. Fanon states: "Melouza and Wagram developed, to an ultimate point of cruelty, methods in which rapes and massacres ostensibly perpetuated by the FLN, clean-ups of entire *douars*, were aimed at provoking the outrage of the population and the condemnation of the revolutionary movement." (Fanon 1967 pg. 59). The colonizer was brutally attacking the villages/douars of the minorities and blaming the FLN for these brutal massacres. Again, the emphasis is on fomenting an Algerian on Algerian war to the benefit of the colonizer. The quest was then to foster the formation and growth of an alternate Algerian political movement to the FLN and in its quest the colonizer fixated on the Algerian Nationalist Movement (MNA), which had relevance and traction on the ground only in the minds of the colonizers. Fanon states: "Colonialism's trump card, however, was represented by the MNA. Non-existent on the national territory, Messalism in France enjoyed the enemy's unconditional support. The French on a number of occasions facilitated the transport of hundreds of Messalists and undertook to arm them." (Fanon 1967 pg. 60). The anti-colonizer movement of Algeria was now involved in a fratricidal war where the adherents of Messalism were now dependent on the colonizer's support to wage war on the FLN in Algeria, another political movement to emerge from the discourse of Messalism. A schism within Algerian anti-colonial discourse was now serving the interests of the colonizer adding further support by the masses to the FLN, who absorbed or eliminated the fighters transported to Algeria by the colonizer. There was then need for a third stage which unleashed a geopolitical strategy to expand a war of liberation against colonial domination into an assault on North Atlantic interests by communism through its Algerian instrument, the FLN, and to intervene into the affairs of key Arab allies of the Algerian Revolution, in this case Egypt and the Suez Canal invasion. Fanon states: "The communist scarecrow was not extensively invoked. The French colonialists sensed that it was besides the mark. They were not convinced by the argument." (Fanon 1967 pg. 61). The USA was not convinced by, nor interested in the argument, hence its collapse as an instrument to mobilize US support for the colonizer's war against Algerian liberation.

Fanon continues his analysis of the French colonial strategy to defeat the Algerian war of liberation as follows: "Isolated on the national territory, without any contact with the Algerian people, France adopts positions that are less and less concrete, and more and more illusory." "Wishes are formulated, hypothesis are put forth, and in accordance with a well-known logic these are transformed into elements of reality." (Fanon 1967 pg. 62). The white colonizer must be alienated from the Algerian masses, as the white colonizer views herself/himself as being separate and apart from the non-white colonized masses exerting hegemony over these masses. The white colonizer can only view the masses through their white supremacist prism and formulate discourse which cannot resonate with the masses in rebellion. The white colonizer can only dominate and exert hegemony through their military superiority, coupled with the complicity of sections of the colonized. Colonized acceptance and complicity with colonial domination is vital to sustainable colonial domination. Having lost effective, strategic complicity of sections of the Algerian population, the inability of the colonizer to understand the reality of the masses and formulate and unleash discourse necessary to disarm the masses at the level of the idea was catastrophic. Truth formulated by the colonizer was not resonating with the masses as the truth of the Revolution was rapidly becoming paramount. Fanon continues: "But meeting reality face to face requires other techniques. Escape into the world of desires, into futile outbursts of anger, does not constitute a solution to the Franco-Algerian war." "The chimera of possible dissensions shows a possible total absence of critical sense since of course the reality does not seem to conform to those visions or to those desires." (Fanon 1967 pg. 62). The white colonizer is in need of a solution to ensure that the Franco-Algerian war is resolved in her/his favor, but they lack the instruments in their discourse to unravel and understand the revolutionary reality on the ground. They then employ flights of fancy as instruments of understanding which manufacture a reality in their image and likeness on the ground, thereby using chimeras as the basis of their truth. This is the process which can only proffer the Final Solution as the means to an end. Fanon states: "Without any grasp of reality, unable or unwilling to recognize the Algerian national will and to draw the inescapable logical conclusion, the French authorities today live under the domination of desires and prophecies." (Fanon 1967 pg. 65). The desire to exert hegemony over colonized Algeria is unstinting as it's their entitlement as French members of the only master race on Earth: the whites. Prophecies made by secular and Christian white supremacy insist that colonized Algeria is white entitlement/privilege to so exploit as they desire. White desire and prophecy, all the products of the discourse of white supremacy, are sufficient, definitive reasons to wage war on Algeria towards decimating the non-white population with the aim of ensuring white hegemony.

Fanon's analysis of the colonizer's strategy to break the back of the Algerian rebellion in 1957 is of acute relevance to an analysis of the strategy of the Algerian revolutionary elite to evolve into a revolutionary oligarchy, whilst exerting sustainable hegemony over the Algerian masses. The relevance of Fanon's analysis of 1957 points to the reality that the core issue is power and power relations and how the revolutionary elite utilized the strategy of the colonizer to appropriate power unto itself whilst simultaneously alienating the masses from power. When faced with the first effective challenge to their hegemonic power in the 1990's, the revolutionary oligarchy unleashed the Final Solution, justifying this with the imminent threat of Islamic Extremism to the revolution. The revolutionary elite cultivated their collaborators, separated them from the masses, insisted that the elite/oligarchy was the revolution and applied the colonial strategy to divide the masses into races, ethnicities and clans at war with each other.

Torture as an Instrument of Colonial Power

This article was published in El Moudjahid, No. 10, September 1957, where Fanon deals with the nature of the colonizer's instrument of power, torture, in Algeria towards breaking the back of the Algerian Revolution. Fanon states: "In reality, the attitude of the French troops in Algeria fits into a pattern of police domination, of systematic racism, of dehumanization rationally pursued. Torture is inherent in the whole colonialist configuration." (Fanon 1965 pg. 64). When the hegemony of the discourse of white supremacy is under attack by non-whites there is only one possible response that this discourse can generate: violence against the non-white race constituted by the white supremacist worldview. In this white supremacist apocalyptic vision of white power, torture is the most expressive instrument unleashed to write on the bodies/minds of the non-white race the power of the master race. Torture becomes an issue when used on white bodies/minds, but never an issue when unleashed on non-white bodies/minds as they present grave threats by their very being, existence and presence; from African enslavement, the conquest of the First Peoples to the War on Terror of the 21st century.

Fanon now presents the Algerian Revolution as the dialectical antithesis of colonial domination. Is Algeria in the 21st century the synthesis that was the outcome of the clash between colonial domination and the Algerian Revolution or is it in fact a betrayal of the antithesis of colonial domination? The manner in which Fanon describes his antithesis is the guide towards interrogating his choice of historical/dialectical materialism as an adequate descriptor of 21st Algerian reality. Fanon states: "The Algerian Revolution, by proposing the liberation of the national territory, is aimed both at the death of this configuration and at the creation of a new society. The independence of Algeria is not only the death of this colonialism, but the disappearance, in this part of the world, of a gangrene germ and of a source of epidemic. The liberation of the Algerian national territory is a defeat for racism and for the exploitation of man; it inaugurates the unconditional reign of justice." (Fanon 1965 pg. 64). Fanon's antithesis will then erase the cancer of colonial domination from the landscape of Algeria, establishing in its place the reign of justice where the exploitation of man by man ends, racism is exorcised from the new Algeria as all the injustices of colonial domination are. In 21st century Algeria there is a new society compared to the colonial order and that which existed before colonial conquest but this new order is certainly not rooted in the reign of justice, the end of exploitation of man by man and the exorcising of the injustice common to the colonial and pre-colonial orders. The synthesis is then simply business as usual in a neo-colonial order presenting all the symptoms of the neo-colonial condition. Algeria and the course of its Revolution to the 21st century falsifies the theory of dialectical materialism, thereby indicating the crisis of Fanon's worldview of Revolution as an absolute even before his untimely death.

Fanon now addresses the widespread support of the masses of France for the colonizer's war against the Algerian Revolution indicating the crisis of discourse sweeping over Fanon and his worldview. Fanon is utilizing the methodology of dialectical/historical materialism, whilst recognizing simultaneously that the workers and peasants of France are not wellsprings of revolution as molded by dialectical materialism. Both the workers/proletariat of Marx and Engels and the peasants of Lenin and Mao Zedong, of France in 1957 are active racists in support of the white colonizer in Algeria. The supposed 'revolutionary classes' destined to be the driving force of history according to historical materialism in France are in fact constituted by the discourse of white supremacy, not the absolute of historical/dialectical materialism. How then can you simultaneously reject this fundamental discursive construct of historical/dialectical materialism, whilst still using its methodology as an analytical tool and embracing its concept of the Revolution derived from historical materialism as an absolute? This places Fanon in an elite club of the colonized who made revolution as Mao Zedong, Fidel Castro, Che Guevara, Amilcar Cabral, Samora Machel and Ho Chi Minh utilizing what discursive tools were at hand, and in their era the white Enlightenment defined the debate, illustrating the hegemony of white discourse over the ideas at that time. Fanon states: "The generalized, and sometimes truly bloody enthusiasm that has marked the participation of the French workers and peasants in the war against the Algerian people has shaken to the foundation the myth of an effective opposition between the people and the government." "The war in Algeria is being waged conscientiously, by all Frenchmen" (Fanon 1965 pg. 65). White solidarity in France, in the face of the assault on white power in Algeria, embraces the so-called revolutionary classes of mainstream and other lines of dialectical/historical materialism. There is then no opposition to the colonial enterprise and the war to hold on to colonial Algeria in the 1950s. The revolutionary classes are then seeped in and fully immersed by the hegemonic discourse of white supremacy. Fanon continues: "But the colonial reconquest in its essence, the armed expedition, the attempt to throttle the liberty of a people, are not condemned." (Fanon 1965 pgs. 65-66). The complicity of the so-called revolutionary classes with the white colonial re-conquest falsifies historical materialism, whilst illustrating the potency of the discourse of white supremacy in constituting the worldview of white folks.

Fanon then deals with the whites who support the colonial re-conquest, but deplore the use of torture as an instrument of power to effect re-conquest. To support colonial re-conquest automatically registers as an approbation for the use of any and all means to attain a successful reconquest. The support of colonial reconquest, but the rejection of the instrument of torture is a contradiction in terms as torture is a necessary instrument for the success of the colonial conquest and reconquest. This then is a ploy, a political and geopolitical instrument designed to distinguish its proponents from the bland mass of support for colonial reconquest. Fanon states: "One cannot both be in favor of the maintenance of French domination in Algeria and opposed to the means that this maintenance requires." "Colonialism cannot be understood without the possibility of torturing, of violating, or of massacring. Torture is an expression and a means of the occupant-occupied relationship." (Fanon 1965 pg. 66). The occupant-occupied relationship is a power relationship where the occupant is constituted by the hegemonic discourse of white supremacy. This discourse frames the nature of the worldview of the white occupier, which constitutes the occupied for the white occupier and it is this white supremacist discourse that manufactures torture of the occupied as an instrument of power of the occupier and a living expression of the nature of the power relation between occupier-occupied. Torture expresses the power of the white occupier over the non-white occupied, whilst being a tool to ensure compliance of the occupied with the hegemony of the white occupant. In the neo-colonial condition there is no occupant-occupied relationship as this is replaced with the dominator-dominated relationship, within the context of a world order of free, sovereign nations. Under this order the hegemon is the USA which has illustrated in the 21st century its ability and willingness to weaponize its instruments of financial and economic domination to assault the nations it named as potent threats to its world hegemony. This is the first instrument of genocide now unleashed in the 21st century through financial and economic sanctions. The second instrument of power is the military might of the USA, which is now allied with assaults of the first order to ensure the US hegemony over the world order driven by the discourse of white supremacy.

In his analysis of torture in the Franco-Algerian war, Fanon presents a statement which reveals the use of the Islamic discourse of Jihad and the primacy of the Shahid in Jihad as an instrument of the Revolution towards mobilization of the Islamic masses and attaining legitimation of the revolutionary war by encasing it in Islamic discourse. The revolutionary elite was then manipulating Islamic discourse as an instrument of its hegemony over the masses, which with victory was even more necessary to realize their quest to become an oligarchy. Fanon is writing on the actions of the revolutionary forces that effectively stymied the actions of the French police in their application of torture to the masses as follows: "The multiple appearance of dynamic revolutionary bodies, the lightning reaction of our *fidayines,* the spread of the FLN throughout the national territory, confronted the French police with insurmountable obstacles." (Fanon 1965 pg. 67). The discourse of Jihad and the primacy of the Shahid was incorporated into the fighting mechanism of the FLN, which meant that to the Muslim viewer this was not a revolutionary movement averse to Islam and those fighters designated Shahid who subsequently died in battle will be honored in the Islamic manner by their family and the social group/s they came from. This quest for legitimation through utilization of the discourse of Jihad set in train the movement within the Revolution that effectively made its challenge for power by constitutional means in the 1990s and was violently suppressed. The most potent instance of legitimacy the revolutionary elite claimed for itself was the embrace of Jihad and the Shahid to then abrogate revolutionary power onto itself stored in the hands of the oligarchy, turning its back on its obligation to the Muslim masses created by the sacrifice of the Shahids. This refusal to honor one's obligation culminated in the movement of the 1990s.

Fanon's presentation on torture now reveals the core aspect of the occupant-occupied and the dominator-dominated relationships which is subservience at the level of the idea, where there is no hegemony without dominance at the level of the idea. In both power relations, discourse will be manufactured to seduce and deceive those dominated and occupied, even more so in the 21st century where the dominated live off truths manufactured by the oligarchs to ensure the integrity of the world system of US hegemony in this era of digital technology. Fanon states: "After having denied the existence of torture in Algeria, the French have used a double argument. First of all, it was claimed, the cases are exceptional. The most serious abdication of the French intellectuals is having tolerated this lie." "This second argument is an important one. It shows both the cynicism of the French authorities and the growing impossibility of cheating, of dissimulating, of lying. The French, for one whole year, have constantly repeated that only former S.S. soldiers serving in the Foreign Legion are responsible for the torture." (Fanon 1965 pgs. 67-68). The democracies of the North Atlantic exhibit the reality of political mobilization and governance premised on manufactured truth geared to seduce the electorate. The issue is not the lies, nor the lies exposed in a democracy but the political resonance of the manufactured truths. What the dominator does to ensure white hegemony is the only valid truth, which is spun to the electorate of the specific North Atlantic state and the world audience in real time through manufactured truths to purchase their servility. The Revolution had its own truth on torture which has hegemony only in Algeria, for there was no opposition to the manufactured truth in France as a result of white solidarity. Fanon insists that in this scenario the ends becomes detached from the means as the flood of manufactured truths focus on the ends in order to mask the means, overdetermining the ends whilst liberating the means from the strategic imperative. You then get war for war's sake and torture for the personal fun of the torturer, which adequately describes the pathway of the discourse of white supremacy since the declaration of the War on Terror in the early 21st century. Fanon states: "In this perspective, in which the excuse of the end tends more and more to become detached from the means, it is normal for torture to become its own justification. And the colonialist system, in order to be logical, must be prepared to claim torture as one of its important elements." (Fanon 1965 pg. 69). In the War on Terror of the 21st century, the excuses of the ends have enabled the detachment of the means from the strategic ends, where torture is now claimed as a necessary and logical means to ensure the integrity of the hegemony of the USA over the world system of the 21st century. The occupant-occupied power relation is now non-hegemonic replaced by the dominator-dominated power relation in a geopolitical context, but the hegemony of the discourse of white supremacy continues, which drove the colonial power relation, and today in the 21st century drives the geopolitical dominator-dominated power relation in the context of neo-liberal financial markets capitalism. The manner of composing a threat posed to white supremacist hegemony and formulating the strategy to end that threat remains from colonial domination to 21st century world hegemony, non-white genocide as there can only be one, the master race. In the 21st century a menu of instruments of power has now been formulated and unleashed towards immersing an enemy nation with waves of impacts intent on genocide in a slow, grinding process that wears down the inferior race, where they reach the point of begging for the relief of death. Whilst the real expectation of imminent death through weapons of mass destruction rubs salt in your wounds. This is a spectacle of white power last seen under white colonial power now reformulated for the 21st century. Hence Fanon's relevance to the 21st century and the necessity of this series.

In ending his article Fanon deals with the rejection of specific means to the end of colonial reconquest utilized in Algeria as being contrary to a concept of French national honor, which in itself is a product of the discourse of white supremacy through its supplicant discourse of white, French nationalism and the body of myths that define and drive it. Fanon states: "The gravity of the tortures, the horror of the rape of little Algerian girls, are perceived because their existence threatens a certain idea of French honor." "Such shutting out of the Algerian, such ignoring of the tortured man or of the massacred family, constitute a wholly original phenomenon. It belongs to that form of egocentric, sociocentric thinking which has become the characteristic of the French." (Fanon 1965 pg. 71). Of the wide range of means used to attain the given end in Algeria only specific means are seen and reacted to by segments of the French population, only because these means tarnish the mythic honor of the French nation/race. The Algerian and the barbarism unleashed on them by the French are simply not seen, the reality does not register on French consciousness for this is not barbarity, this is defense of the entitlement of the race, of race privilege. The Algerians are non-whites, non-human, deserving of everything they receive for daring to challenge the hegemony of the master race over them. This is then the worldview of a race of sociopaths, a sociopathic race constituted by the discourse of white supremacy. The combination of being egocentric with being sociocentric constituted by the discourse of white supremacy results in a sociopathic white supremacist with a propensity for genocide of non-white races. The living embodiment of this worldview and the personality constituted to effect it was the police agent in Algeria charged with breaking the back of the revolution. Fanon states: "What these police agents were looking for was not so much a moral assuagement as the possibility of resuming the tortures." "The police agent who tortures in Algeria infringes no law. His act fits into the framework of the colonial institution." (Fanon 1965 pg. 71). The white supremacist police agent has to get on with the strategically necessary task at hand, which will be attained by any means necessary for there is no law in Algeria limiting white, colonizer instruments of power. There is no rule of law in occupied Algeria, only the hegemony of white power. This is the message of 21st century white supremacist USA to its internal non-white races and the non-white nations of the world geopolitical order, that there is no rule of law to limit USA's white power projected internally and externally. Non-white lives internally and externally simply cannot matter when white hegemony is challenged by non-whites as China breeding visions of the white apocalypse. Fanon ends the article as follows: "The Algerian people are not unaware of the fact that the colonialist structure rests on the necessity of torturing, raping, and committing massacres. And for this reason the demand that we make-our objective-is from the outset total and absolute." (Fanon 1967 pg. 72). The only solution to the colonial domination of Algeria and all it entails is the totalist absolute of Revolution as formulated by the left of the white enlightenment. But a totalist absolute is a schizophrenic entity as it speaks to justice, the end of exploitation of man by man and the masses wielding power in a new social order, whilst the power relations of this totalist absolute demand and enable a revolutionary elite to collect hegemonic power, during the daily grind of the revolution in action over the masses and the process. With victory over the occupant/colonizer, the colonial state is captured by this revolutionary elite and transformed into the instruments of power of this elite, which they will then use to grow themselves into a hegemonic oligarchy dominating the post-colonial social order. We have then burdened ourselves with white discursive concepts to free ourselves from white colonial domination, which then enables a new order of domination premised on non-whites exercising local, immediate hegemony which fits perfectly into the neo-colonial condition which at its core is premised on white geopolitical and economic domination. The problem then is the discourse of the Revolution formulated by the white Enlightenment rooted in the discursive concept of the totality, the whole, that is an absolute, which is an essentially totalitarian concept rooted in white supremacy. In this totality, whole, the sum of the individuals plus trumps the rights and freedom of the individual, for the individual only has rights and freedom that are organic to the totality, the whole, which is a discourse that exalts and worships power and those who wield it, not individual rights and freedom. The Algerian masses supported Revolution but all did not embrace totalist and absolute Revolution because for many the Revolution embraced salient tenets of Islamic discourse, especially the discourse of Jihad and the primacy of the Shahid. In the 1990s the choice of the Islamic alternative to totalist, absolute Revolution as animated by the revolutionary oligarchy was made manifest and the masses paid the price for this as demanded by totalist, absolute Revolution.

The totalist absolute Revolution and Fanon's Dilemma

In three articles that appeared in three issues of El Moudjahid of December 1, 15 and 30, 1957, Fanon deals with the position of the French left and democrats on the Algerian Revolution. Fanon is articulating a discourse of Revolution that is the product of the white Enlightenment of Europe, whilst whites of France of the left and the democrats are exhibiting the symptoms of white solidarity that contradicts their publicly declared worldviews. Fanon is then in a precarious position as white supremacy trumps the discourse of the totalist absolute Revolution and the discourse of the rights of man expressed in a democracy. Fanon states: "Because it has no hold on the people, the democratic Left, shut in upon itself, convinces itself in endless articles and studies that Bandung has sounded the death knell of colonialism." (Fanon 1965 pgs. 76-77). The democratic left has no grounding with the masses, as they exist for themselves and by themselves. More than that they have convinced themselves that revolution is not necessary to end colonial domination as there is an anti-colonial momentum sweeping the world, seen in the Bandung conference. This leftist line cannot and will not support the Algerian Revolution, nor oppose the French war of reconquest. This then is a compromised position which reveals the power of white solidarity in the face of a non-white assault on white entitlement. Fanon continues: "But all this knowledge proves futile because it is utterly disproportionate to the simple ideas current among the people." (Fanon 1967 pg. 77). The French left has placed the generation of knowledge in a crypt, thereby alienated from the masses and having no impact on the ideas of the masses on the Algerian

Revolution. By offering no alternative at the level of the idea, the left has allowed colonial discourse to mold the opinion of the masses on the Algerian Revolution. The French left is then a stranger to the daily reality of the Algerian masses, which is worse than its alienation from the French masses. This daily reality of the Algerian masses demands Revolution, which means that the French left is a fetter on the progress of the Algerian masses. Fanon states: "The only possible issue, the sole way of salvation for this people is to react as energetically as it can to the genocide campaign being conducted against it. The reaction is becoming progressively more absolute." (Fanon 1967 pg. 78). The French colonizer has applied an absolute, genocide, to break the back of the Algerian, non-white war against the white, French colonizer. This absolute unleashed is in keeping with the nature of white colonization, which demands the unleashing of an absolute by the Algerian masses to match and counter the colonial absolute. The only absolute that fits the bill is Revolution and those of the left who refuse to accept the need for this absolute are in fact insisting that the Algerian masses accept genocide unleashed by the colonizer and surrender to French colonial re-conquest.

Fanon now analyses the support of the French nation for the war for the reconquest of Algeria and the context opposition to this war now finds itself in, hence the absence of opposition in France. Fanon states: "Here we encounter a double phenomenon. First of all an ultra-chauvinistic, nationalistic, patriotic propaganda, mobilizing the implicit racist elements of the collective consciousness of the colonialist people, introduces a new element. It immediately becomes obvious that it is no longer possible to back the the colonized without at the same time opposing the national solution. The fight against colonialism becomes a fight against the nation. The war of reconquest is assumed by the colonialist country as a whole, and anti-colonialist arguments lose their efficacy, become abstract theories and finally disappear from the democratic literature." (Fanon 1967 pg. 78). To oppose colonial domination, to oppose the war of colonial reconquest of Algeria is to oppose the very existence of the nation of France and French nationalism. For the nation, French nationalism and French colonial domination are all instruments of the discourse of white supremacy, where the white nation is a mythic totality, a whole which encompasses a nationality of the master race endowed by god and nature with inalienable entitlement exercised through conquest of inferior non-white races. For the white left of France to oppose colonial domination is in effect to oppose themselves in their white skins animated with their white supremacist worldview, to oppose the white nation and to commit race suicide. White race suicide is unthinkable for that is an instrument of power formulated for conquered non-white races by white supremacist discourse. Being white at all times first, the solution is to simply dump the leftist chatter for a pragmatic position that preserves your race integrity. Fanon continues: "The accusation of treason to which the adversaries of the Algerian war exposed themselves became a formidable weapon in the hands of the French government. Thus in early 1957 many democrats ceased their protests or were overwhelmed by the clamor for vengeance, and a clumsily structured elementary patriotism manifested itself steeped in racism-violent, totalitarian, in short, fascist. The French government was to find its second argument in what is called terrorism." "The concept of barbarism appeared and it was decided that France in Algeria was fighting barbarism." (Fanon 1967 pg. 79). The French government of the day was now punishing dissent against the war of colonial reconquest accusing the opposition in France of treason against the nation and the race. This desire to police dissent formulated a fascist patriotism which silenced the opposition. Power in its perpetual power relation with the rule of law trumps law by manufacturing a crisis of law and order, which enables power to wield the force it possesses. Democracy founded on the rule of law is then a mythic instrument of power, easily surmounted by crises of order generated by power relations. The French government then plays the terrorism card which utilizes the imagery of a non-white race killing white folks devoid of context, for context with white folks is irrelevant when dealing with non-whites. The white blood lust drives the need for revenge, for graphic barbarous retaliation where one white life is worth multiples of dead non-whites. The designation of non-whites as terrorists, purveyors of terrorism and barbarism now gives the white barbaric backlash justification and resonance with the discourse of white supremacy. France is then fighting a just war against terrorism and barbarism in Algeria.

Welcome to the War on Terror of the 21st century driven by the discourse of white supremacy. The French left simply capitulated to this assault by the white state by first insisting to the Algerian revolution that terrorist acts must be stopped, but greeted the acts of the colonizer's war of reconquest with silence. Fanon states: "In France it becomes less and less clear why the Algerian war must end. People forget more and more that France, in Algeria, is trampling popular sovereignty underfoot, flouting the right of people to self-determination, murdering thousands of men and women. In France, among the left, the Algerian war is tending to become a disease of the French system, like ministerial instability, and colonial wars a nervous tic with which France is afflicted, a part of the national panorama, a familiar detail." (Fanon 1967 pgs. 79-80). The discourse of white supremacy can only see and react to threats posed by non-white races to white hegemony over the world. White domination of the non-white world is an entitlement and all are expected to accept, be servile, docile and comply. To dare to resist is to resist the natural order of white hegemony and you will be broken by any means necessary. Rights of man, self-determination, sovereignty are all concepts formulated for the political wars within the white race, they simply cannot and don't apply to us when we are dealing with white hegemony/ white power. The primary issue is exerting hegemony over the non-white races of the world through domination of the geopolitical expressions of these races as nation states. French white people can never embrace the rights of the Algerian to self-determination, for an inferior race has no such white rights. The left refuses to gaze upon the white supremacy of its worldview by gazing at its French navel, which allows it to be irrelevant to and silent on Algerian reality as it conjures up the systemic facade to mask to itself the white supremacist colonial imperial

adventure that is the French war of colonial reconquest in Algeria. In the 21st century the battle lines are boldly drawn, demarcated and lucidly illustrated, where the message sent is one of hegemonic white power that has no limits in its quest to crush non-white races in their nation states branded as enemies. This expression of white hegemonic power has finally exposed the lie that is the so-called international order constituted by the white world to serve the white world during a kinder, gentler time. Fanon continues on the left: "This attitude of the French intelligentsia must not be interpreted as the consequence of an inner solidarity with the Algerian people. This advice and these criticisms are to be explained by the ill-repressed desire to guide, to direct the very liberation movement of the oppressed." (Fanon 1967 pg. 80). White supremacy intends to retain control in the event of successful wars of liberation against colonial domination and this desire is enabled by the revolutionary elite using white ideas to drive their war of liberation and insisting that the white nations are developed, and we being underdeveloped we need their "expertise." But the only expertise they have is rendering us and keeping us underdeveloped. White supremacists are aware that we remain servile at the level of the idea, hence they insist that we need their expertise, leadership skills and their knowledge base. We must then surrender leadership of our Revolution to white supremacists as we are inferior, incapable races; which we then do, as the Algerian revolutionary elite did. Fanon now states that the French democrat is in fact irrelevant to the politics of the war for re-conquest of Algeria in France. Fanon states: "Thus can be understood the constant oscillation of the French democrats between a manifest or latent hostility and the wholly unreal aspiration to militate 'actively to the end.'Such a confusion indicates a lack of preparation for the facing of concrete problems and a failure on the part of French democrats to immerse themselves in the political life of their own countries." (Fanon 1967 pg. 80). It is not the agenda of the democrats and especially the left of French politics to concern themselves with the reality of French politics and to immerse themselves in the task of being relevant to French politics. It is their agenda to wield influence over, to impact and even to lead the Algerian Revolution, thereby ensuring continued white hegemony over the new Algeria, hence the Algerian neo-colonial condition.

Fanon now exposes the expanse that separates the historical materialist vision of what constitutes a social order in Europe and that of colonial Algeria. Fanon is now presenting his analysis of colonial Algeria which is contrary to that of historical materialism and by extension one expects a concept of Revolution that is relevant to Algeria and alien to that of historical materialism. Fanon states: "At this level, reflection enables us to discover an important peculiarity of colonial reality in Algeria. Within a nation it is usual and commonplace to identify two antagonistic forces: the working class and bourgeois capitalism. In a colonial country this distinction proves totally inadequate. What defines the colonial situation is rather the undifferentiated character that foreign domination presents. The colonial situation is first of all a military conquest continued and reinforced by a civil and police administration. In Algeria, as in every colony, the foreign oppressor looks upon the native as marking a limit to his dignity and defines himself as constituting an irreducible negation of the colonized country's national existence." (Fanon 1967 pg. 80). The colonizer exerts hegemony over the colonized by dint of military conquest, buttressed by the colonial State, where civil and police instruments of power maintain the hegemony of the white colonizer. The dynamic of colonial domination is then based on white, foreign minority domination over a non-white, native majority. It is undifferentiated as the entire social order and its expression on the landscape of the conquered land is premised on a Manichean duality: white/colonizer/dominator versus non-white/colonized/dominated. There is no class structure, no class warfare, hence no revolutionary potential arising from class struggle. Revolution has to be premised on the non-white majority expelling by force of arms the hegemonic white minority. This Revolution has the task of dealing with white domination at the material level and at the level of the idea, the person, the personality and the worldview. Because in the power relation of colonizer and colonized, the white colonizer viewed the non-white colonized as a limit to her/his white power, to his dignity as master race of the world, to untrammeled enjoyment of her/his right to manifest destiny and right arising from conquest. The white has then to constantly formulate and unleash instruments by which to dominate the non-whites of the world in order for the master race to self-actualize their manifest destiny. The master race must then be forever plagued with thoughts of the Final Solution for they are a minority race driven paranoid schizophrenic with their fear of a non-white planet. The master race must constantly pursue the dream of negating irreducibly the expressions of our national existence. They threw away colonization when it was no longer feasible, formulating and unleashing

the neo-colonial condition and in the 21st century they have now embraced the methodology of a proto-enslavement mode of domination within the neo-colonial condition. This is what constitutes the need for an irreducible negation as we, the non-white races of the world in the worldview of the discourse of white supremacy present by our very physical existence a grave, existential threat to the white folks constituted by the discourse of white supremacy. This need is then only satisfied with genocide/cleansing of the non-whites. Fanon then comes to this conclusion arising from the Manichean duality of white/non-white in Algeria as follows: "The status of the foreigner, the conqueror, of the French man in Algeria, is the status of an oppressor. The Frenchman in Algeria cannot be neutral or innocent. Every Frenchman in Algeria oppresses, despises, dominates." (Fanon 1967 pg. 81). In this Manichean duality the skin of both locked in the power relation is their sin, creating a chasm of separation where the liberation of the majority/non-white can only be accomplished by defeating and expelling the minority/white from the occupied terrain of Algeria. This defeat and expulsion must take place at the level of the idea, the personality, the worldview, physically and materially. The neo-colonial condition is then the mechanism formulated to enable the end of formal colonial domination, replaced by economic/financial, military, ideational and psychological domination in national territories that are free of the white colonizer, replaced by the white expert, the foreign investor and the aid officials.

Fanon having thrashed the relevance of historical materialism as a tool of analysis of white colonial domination returns to the manner in which the French democrats play with the nature of French domination of Algeria. Fanon states: "French democrats in deciding to give the name 'colonialism' to what has never ceased to be military conquest and occupation, have deliberately simplified facts. The term of colonialism created by the oppressor is too affective, too emotional. It is placing a national problem on a psychological level. This is why, as conceived by these democrats, the contrary of colonialism is not the recognition of the right of peoples to self-determination, but the necessity on an individual level, for less racial, more open, more liberal types of behavior. Colonialism is not a type of individual relations but the conquest of a national territory and the oppression of a people, that is all. It is not a certain type of human behavior or a pattern of relations between individuals." (Fanon 1967 pg. 80). The French democrats have formulated a discourse of colonialism which masks the white supremacist dynamic that drives colonial conquest, occupation, domination and oppression. Hence colonialism is a specific type of individual relations devoid of race imagery and supremacy, therefore it only plagues specific types of white folks, whilst the French democrats are free of infection. The Algerian revolution can then trust the French democrats, learn from them and embrace them in the new dispensation for Algeria. This discourse of colonialism of the French democrats pervades the neo-colonial condition, where the former colonized non-whites embrace their ex-colonial master as their new benefactors as they are now free citizens of sovereign states in a commonwealth of nations. In this environment the white colonizer is absolved of all past and present sins as the free people of these sovereign states are the ones to blame for the arrested development of the former colonies of the white colonizer. This is a discourse to disarm recognition of the hegemony of the discourse of white supremacy in the course of actions adopted by the whites of the North Atlantic both past and present. Fanon continues: "The Algerian people have proved refractory to the over-simple imagery according to which the colonialist is a special type of man who can be readily recognized. Thus it has been claimed that all Frenchmen in Algeria are not colonialists, and that there are different degrees of colonialism." "French colonialism, French oppression in Algeria, form a common whole which does not necessarily require the existence of Mr. Borgeaud. French domination is the totality of the forces that are opposed to the existence of the Algerian nation, and for the Algerian, concretely, Mr. Blachette is no more 'colonialist' than a police officer, a rural policeman or a school teacher." (Fanon 1967 pg. 82). Fanon expresses his concept of the white occupier/colonizer within the ideational ambit of the white man's concept of the whole and the totality, thereby placing him on a trajectory where the white man's concept of the absolute of revolution that is a totality and a whole is the only instrument possible to defeat white colonial occupation. When you dance in the white man's discourse, you can only see the problems the discourse uncovers and the solutions the discourse formulates. But this is a white supremacist discourse which can never formulate solutions to white hegemony over non-white races. The concepts of totality and the whole were formulated and continue to be utilized to frame white hegemony over non-white races. When embraced and utilized by non-white races it is embraced by those elements intent on growing themselves into an oligarchy, on justifying their hegemony over the masses. The history of the neo-colonial condition illustrates that those who embrace these concepts plunder their nation for their own benefit, impoverish the masses of the nation and are willing, servile supplicants of the white North Atlantic hegemon. Fanon's dilemma and his nakedness is potently exposed by his embrace of these two lynch-pin racist concepts of the North Atlantic and of the inherent nature of the revolutionary elite of Algeria. Fanon continues: "French domination is the totality of the forces that are exposed to the existence of the Algerian nation," "The Algerian experiences French colonialism as an undifferentiated whole, not out of simple mindedness or xenophobia but because in reality every Frenchman in Algeria maintains, with reference to the Algerian, relations that are based on force." (Fanon 1967 pg. 82). Fanon's colonizer totality and whole is rooted and premised in force relations where a totality of force, a whole premised on force relations is the basis of and enables a white, minority invasive race to exert hegemony over a non-white majority. This is then a totality of domination and oppression that benefits only the white invasive minority, a whole constituted by force exerted by a minority over a majority. There is then no shared values, no society, no social order, no consensus, no functionality premised on the needs of the society, there are no classes and class struggle. The totality and whole of force is an absolute that can only be destroyed by an absolute, Revolution, which then constitutes the hegemony of the revolutionary oligarchy premised on the neo-colonial totality of force. Fanon states: "Colonialism is the organization of the domination of a nation after military conquest. The war of liberation is not a seeking for reforms but the grandiose effort of a people, which had been mummified, to rediscover its own genius, to re-assume its history and assert its sovereignty." (Fanon 1967 pgs. 83-84). The colonial totality of force mummifies the masses, submerges the genius of the colonized with the colonial psycho-existential complex, freezes native history, history made by the masses to the pre-colonial conquest period for under colonial domination we don't make history it is made for us as it is his story, the story of the white colonizer who formulates history for us. The colonial whole, its totality of force results in a people without sovereignty, without destiny made by us as it is made for us by the colonizer. Servile suppliants we are. What then has changed in the 21st century under the neo-colonial condition, oh yes, we are free!

Fanon now deals with the French vision of Algeria arising from its military conquest and occupation of Algeria, a vision entirely different from the position held on Africa south of the Sahara and other parts of the French Empire. Fanon describes this French vision of Algeria as being rooted in mystification of Algeria and all that it represented to French white supremacy.

Fanon states: "When one closely examines the colonial relations that have existed between Algeria and France one notes that the Algerian territory, by the very characteristics of the conditions of its conquest, has always represented for France a real prolongation. At no time has France indicated in identical terms its property rights over Africa south of the Sahara, or over any other fragment of the 'French Empire.'" "France's right in Africa was based rather on a right of property, whereas in Algeria, from the beginning, relations of identity were affirmed." (Fanon 1967 pg. 84). French nationalist white supremacy insisted that by dint of white conquest of the inferior races of Algeria, white supremacist domination of Algeria through various instruments of power will never end but prolongated across time and space. Algeria was not a property right by dint of conquest but part of French nationalist white supremacist identity and to lose it, whether by the gift of independence or Revolution, was unthinkable. Loss of Algeria will do grave damage to French nationalist white supremacy as the mythic ethos of the white nation will be debased and exposed in all its weakness, especially since the debacle of the second world war and the loss of Indochina. White supremacist mystification in the 1950s was the instrument of mass mobilization utilized by the politicians and the oligarchs of France to whip up mass support for their war of reconquest of Algeria. Fanon continues: "Never was the principle according to which no one can enslave another so wholly true. After having domesticated the Algerian people for more than a century, France finds herself a prisoner of her conquest and incapable of detaching herself from it, of defining new relations, of making a fresh start." (Fanon 1967 pg. 85). French nationalist white supremacy, that is hegemonic, cannot walk away from Algeria which amounts to surrender of the master race to an inferior race nor can it accept Algeria dominated by the

neo-colonial condition. Mystification demands in the 20th century, in spite of pressing geo-political realities of the day, that France unleash genocide on the Algerians in order for France to retain control of the geographic expression of Algeria. For France is not the France defined by nationalist white supremacy without possession of Algeria. As the USA is not the USA defined by

nationalist white supremacy in the 21st century without world hegemony.

Fanon now returns to the position of the French left on Algeria which indicates their white supremacist worldview and the race solidarity that flows from this position. Fanon states: "If we examine the attitude of the French Left with reference to the objective of our struggle, we perceive that no faction admits the possibility of a real national liberation." "Such positions clearly manifest that even the so called extremist parties consider that France has rights in Algeria and that the lightening of domination does not necessarily imply the disappearance of every link. This mental attitude assumes the guise of a technocratic paternalism, of a disingenuous warning against the danger of regression." (Fanon 1967 pgs. 87-88). The French left, in its entire diversity, does not and cannot accept the possibility of Algerian victory over the French in Algeria. To accept this possibility of a non-white race gaining victory over France is unthinkable, hence their only position is that it is an impossibility, hence the Algerian revolution is misguided, illusory and destined to fail with grave consequences for the Algerian masses. The Algerian Revolution is then portrayed by the French left as a regressive, futile action which will take Algeria back to pre-colonial, Islamic barbarism. French colonial domination is then modernity and progress for Algeria and what should constitute the revolution is the continued embrace of France under new terms of endearment. The French left is then revealed as unapologetically white supremacist and is demanding continued French paternalistic hegemony over Algeria, at the level of the idea at minimum.

Fanon now presents his concept of the neo-colonial condition as follows: "The French democrats do not always perceive the colonialist or-to use the new concept-the neo-colonialist character of their attitude. The demand for special links with France is a response to the desire to maintain colonial structures intact. What is involved here is a type of terrorism of necessity on the basis of which it is decided that nothing valid can be conceived or achieved in Algerian independence of France. In fact, the demand for special links with France comes down to a determination to maintain Algeria eternally in the stage of a minor and protected State. But also to a determination to guarantee certain forms of exploitation of the Algerian people." (Fanon 1967 pg. 88). The desire is to maintain white supremacist domination of the state of Algeria, its oligarchs, politicians and the masses without need for the old colonial structures and power relations. That is the new model of white supremacist hegemony being championed by the French left which makes it progressive, the evolutionary product of a discourse of white supremacy that is evolving to ensure the sustainable hegemony of white supremacy in a new geopolitical reality. This progressive arm of the white Enlightenment evolved rapidly to deal with the success of the Algerian Revolution in defeating the French colonizer setting about the task of ensuring the revolutionary elite became compliant and servile. The door was opened to this progressive wing with the betrayal of the revolution by the revolutionary elite with their quest to grow themselves into an oligarchy, which they successfully did. The lesson is then potently clear that the neo-colonial condition is a power relation we accept and inflict on ourselves as we accept at the level of the idea and make our servility manifest via our actions. What the white folks desire is irrelevant, for as with the slavers of West Africa, our complicity makes it all happen. We condemn ourselves to the self-immolation of hallucinatory whiteness refusing to accept our complicity in our degradation. Fanon returns to the position of the French left as follows: "Because the Left unconsciously obeys the myth of French Algeria, its action does not go beyond aspiring to an Algeria in which more justice would prevail or, at most, an Algeria less directly governed by France. The passion charged chauvinism of French public opinion on the Algerian question exerts pressure on this Left, inclines it to excessive caution, shakes its principles, and places it in a paradoxical and increasingly sterile situation." "Thus the struggle of a people for its independence must be diaphanous if it would enjoy the support of democrats." (Fanon 1967 pg. 89). The French left has but one position which holds to the consensus of France owning Algeria, Algeria as a necessary constituent element of French nationalist white supremacy. But unlike the revolutionary class that the left is supposed to serve and enable in the making of revolution, the left wants a neo-colonial Algeria under French domination, whilst the working class wants colonial Algeria and its boost to French white supremacy and the white race. The French Left is then fettered by the backwardness of this revolutionary working class and by its own adherence to French white supremacy. There is then no revolutionary solidarity with the Algerian revolution naturally occurring and flowing from the French working class and its vanguard, the Left. The Algerian Revolution is then also a revolution against the hegemony of the working class and the left of France and the white world over the revolutionary elite of Algeria. But does the said elite of Algeria view the reality in this way with their commitment to that thing invented by the white Enlightenment for white folks, but appropriated by non-whites and applied to their colonial realities: socialism. The socialism of the revolutionary elite in fact was the instrument of power used to grow themselves into an oligarchy by dominating the masses, thereby killing the Revolution. The Algerian Revolution is anathema to the democrats of France, hence their insistence that their support for the Algerian Revolution is conditional, dependent upon the nature of the Revolution. For support the Revolution must be transparent, translucent and vulnerable as sheer fabric enabling the exertion of French hegemony over the product of the revolution. This is the quest for white supremacist hegemony under the neo-colonial condition when faced with loss of the colony as a result of war. White supremacy trumps all of the discourses of rights and the brotherhood of man, for white is might thus always right, as validated by the geopolitics of the 21st century.

The Specificity of the Algerian Revolutionary

This article was published in El Moudjahid, No. 22, April 16, 1958, where Fanon is discussing in 1958 the strategies adopted by the revolutionary elite which have constituted the Algerian Revolution as a specific, unique event in the history of wars of liberation from colonial domination. Fanon states: "For a variety of reasons, the whole gamut of French public opinion, with rare exceptions, has honored the army, backed the war in Algeria, warned the different governments against unacceptable renunciations in Algeria." "it is surprising that no coherent and effective force has come forward to impose peace on the French colonialists." (Fanon 1967 pg. 99). The French public wants a war of reconquest of Algeria, it does not want anything less than reconquest as there must be no French compromise with the Revolution, for that amounts to surrendering to an inferior race. The embrace of the masses of colonial domination of Algeria has ensured that no political force exists in the politics of France to take power and impose peace in Algeria. This is a battle to the death, where France will engage in battle as long as it is possible to do so. In 1958, France's only path to victory lies in exacting a heavy toll on Algerians for their resistance with the hope that they will abandon the revolution as the price they are paying to attain this end escalates. Therefore, genocide is the path adopted by France in 1958 as this is the ultimate price for resisting the hegemony of white supremacy. Fanon continues: "What has to be said is that with the Algerian war there appeared three phenomena, absolutely new in the struggles for national liberation." (Fanon 1967 pg. 100) The positions of the colonizer and the revolution on their respective strategies to drive the Franco-Algerian war constitutes three new and unique phenomena that distinguish this war of liberation from the rest in this era. Fanon states: "To begin with, at no moment has the FLN appealed to the generosity, to the magnanimity, to the good-nature of the colonizer. In a dizzyingly swift mutation, the colonizer acquires a new quality, which develops in and through combat. The language used by the FLN, from the first days of the Revolution, is a language of authority." "What we ask is that their action be steeped, not in an atmosphere of diffuse sympathy, but in the doctrinal right of an authentic anti-colonialism." (Fanon 1967 pg. 100). The FLN speaks the discourse of Jihad where there is no appeal to the special qualities of the enemy once Jihad has been declared. There can only be the language of imminent victory and what is demanded of the enemy in light of this reality. The FLN embraced and utilized the discourse of Jihad against the colonizer thereby establishing its Islamic credentials with the Algerian masses. This language of Jihad utilized by the Revolution is articulated by Fanon as follows: "The FLN does not aim at achieving a decolonization of Algeria or a relaxation of the oppressive structure. What the FLN demands is the independence of Algeria. An independence which will allow the Algerian people to take its destiny wholly in hand. This objective, this strategy, commands our tactics, our method, and informs the very nature of our struggle." (Fanon 1967 pg. 101). Freedom from the oppression of the kaffirun demands the sacrifice of the masses, including their lives and that of their family. Resistance to the genocide unleashed by the French framed in the language of Jihad. The failure by the revolutionary elite to deliver on the sacrifices made by the masses in keeping with the discourse of Jihad constituted the Islamic alternative in the 1990s which was brutally suppressed by the revolutionary oligarchy. Fanon continues: "The Algerian Revolution has introduced a scandal in the unfolding of the struggles for national liberation. Colonialism generally manages, at the turning-point where history and the nation will reject it, to maintain itself as a value. It is not true that it was a good thing to have made of Algeria what she is today." (Fanon 1967 pg. 101). Even when faced with a war for national liberation the discourse of the colonizer survives as a value infecting the minds of the liberated. Fanon insists that French action in Algeria has made this survival of the worldview of the colonizer problematic at best, if not impossible, hence the scandal constituted by the Revolution. What has in fact been revealed in Algeria is that the values of the colonizer, of white supremacy infected the revolutionary elite and now defines the worldview of the revolutionary oligarchy. This revolutionary elite cum oligarchy is unrelenting in its assaults on the masses to ensure hegemony of these neo-colonial values over the masses in an ongoing attempt to ensure their hegemony.

Fanon continues with his position of the scandal constituted by the total rejection of colonialism by the Algerian Revolution as follows: "French colonialism will not be legitimized by the Algerian people. No spectacular undertaking will makes us forget the legalized racism, the illiteracy, the flunkeyism generated and maintained in the very depth of the consciousness of our people. This is why in our declarations there is never any mention of adaptation, or of alleviation, but of restitution." "That is because by insisting on this national reality, by making of the Revolution of November 1st, 1954, a phase of the popular resistance that began with Abd El Kader, we rob French colonialism of its legitimacy, its would be incorporation into Algerian reality. Instead of integrating colonialism, conceived as the birth of a new world, in Algerian history, we have made of it an unhappy, execrable accident, the only meaning of which was to have inexcusably retarded the coherent evolution of the Algerian society and nation." (Fanon 1967 pg. 101). The only means to expunge the impact of colonizer domination on Algeria is Revolution that delegitimizes and excises from the Algerian psyche the natural order of the colonizer. But the language of the revolution is that of Jihad, for that is the discourse that resonates with the masses on the ground, but not with the worldview of the revolutionary vanguard. The discourse of resistance of the masses is Jihad whilst the revolutionary vanguard articulates to itself white revolutionary secularism seeking to infuse this discourse into the ranks of the disciplined fighting forces under its command with the intention to transform this fighting force, with victory, into the revolutionary army under its hegemony, it primary instrument of power. The discourse of Jihad of the Revolution roots out colonial discourse from the hearts and minds of the masses, but with victory a new battle for the hearts and minds of the masses ensues, as the revolutionary vanguard now wants hegemony as an oligarchy, thereby betraying the Revolution. The white secular revolutionary discourse that the revolutionary vanguard defined themselves by and described as socialist, incubated and insulated the vanguard from the cleansing of the Revolution, which meant that the reputed cleansing was in fact mythic, in keeping with the white secular totalist discourse of socialism that they espoused, in order to mask their blatant intent to ride the backs of the masses to personal power and wealth accumulation. The use of the discourse of Jihad by this vanguard was the potent indicator of a betrayal of the Revolution in the works, as the vanguard did not have any respect for Islamic discourse nor place for it in the Revolution. They were opportunistically exploiting the Islamic worldview of the masses to motivate them to bear and make the great sacrifices as a people necessary to defeat the colonizer. With victory, the vanguard appropriates the spoils of victory for themselves rapidly evolving into a hegemonic oligarchy to the detriment of the masses. The Algerian Revolution illustrates the reality that you can defeat the white colonizer in a war of national liberation which hands power to an oligarchy that has always embraced servility to the white supremacist world order. The war was then necessary to replace the colonizer with the neo-colonial faithful, servile native. Revolution as an absolute is but another white myth swallowed by non-whites, which has purchased the blood of non-whites seeking liberation and unleashed on us a new order of white domination through non-white proxies, for we are free.

Fanon's position on the need for the strategy adopted by the revolutionary elite is further articulated as follows: "The 'nation in the process of becoming,' 'new Algeria,' 'the unique history case,' all these mystifying expressions have been swept away by the position of the FLN and only the heroic combat of a whole people against a century-old oppression has remained in the full sunlight." "Between the break with the Algerian past, entailing as a consequence the acceptance of a renovated but continued colonization, and fidelity to the transitorily subdued nation, the Algerian people has chosen." "There is no new entity born of colonialism. The Algerian people has refused to let the occupation be transformed into collaboration. The French in Algeria have not cohabited with the Algerian people. They have more or less dominated. This is why it was necessary from the beginning to make the French people feel the full scope of our demands." (Fanon 1967 pg. 102). The leadership of the revolutionary vanguard and the sacrifices in combat made by the masses welded into a cohesive unit, a fighting force and citizens of the new, revolutionary Algeria have destroyed the mystified French Algeria, leaving naked in the sunlight, fully exposed French barbarism. The Algerian people has rejected collaboration with the colonizer for revolution, for collaboration illustrates that the masses has accepted the colonizer's position that Algeria's pre- colonial past was one of backward, medieval Islamic stagnation. The rejection of this position of the colonizer meant that the masses identified with their Islamic past as a glorious past into and with which the Revolution flowed in a continuity, hence the war against the colonizer was conceptualized on the ground as Jihad. The Islamic past and its glory then gave meaning to the need for war against France which was the matrix that held the masses together when faced with the barbarity of the French effort to destroy the revolution. Hence the use of the language of Jihad to express the Revolutionary position to the French. There is no new entity born out of colonialism in Algeria as the masses defeated the colonizer on the battlefield giving the French clear choices: they either unleash systematic genocide to destroy the Algerian nation that would tower over the Jewish Holocaust of the Nazis or simply pack up and leave Algeria, which they choose to do. In 1962 when France accepted that their war was lost and national genocide was not on their agenda, they then in keeping with their white supremacist worldview granted independence to what was already free. And so it is reported in white supremacist media

to this day. From 1962 to the 21st century something new has emerged from the Algerian Revolution, which in keeping with Fanon's embrace of white supremacist concepts of absolutes was simply impossible. This is the abrogation of the Revolution by its vanguard, the defanging of the masses by the vanguard and the evolution of the vanguard into an oligarchy. In the context of Fanon's revolution, the vanguard has willingly imposed the neo-colonial condition on the masses of Algeria in the pretext of its quest for modernity and progress as defined by white supremacist discourse. Fanon never lived to experience this crass grab for power and the surrender to white supremacy, but failed to express in his writings on Algeria the readily available signs of the betrayal. Fanon's discourse of the revolution are then convictions against him and the FLN. Fanon states: "From the very beginning the FLN defined its program: to put an end to French occupation, to give the land to the Algerians, to establish a policy of social democracy in which man and woman have an equal right to culture, to material well being and to dignity." (Fanon 1967 pg. 101). The Algerian social order in the 21st century does not reflect the impact of the earnest application of these limited principles, for with victory these principles were interpreted in a manner to enable the hegemony of the revolutionary elite cum oligarchy. For example, social democracy was interpreted as a socialist one party state thereby stifling the attempts of the masses to drive the evolution of revolutionary politics, which included reference to Islamic discourse for models of action. The question then arises of what happened to all the great, unique potential the Algerians developed as a result of revolutionary action from 1954 to 1962 that Fanon describes in detail and insists was real, palpable?

Algeria in the 21st century is then a potent example of raw, naked power/force relations in action in a colonial and revolutionary context that arrives at the same destination as those nations created by a gift of independence from the colonizer, where they never left, they just changed their mode of operations. Revolutionary Algeria then speaks to the strategic importance of an elite/oligarchy exerting hegemony over a social order who willingly embrace white supremacist hegemony as they are servile at the level of the idea. This servility ensures that what was the Revolution according to this elite cum oligarchy was expressed in mythic discourse for the purpose of seduction of the masses. The Revolution was then simply an instrument to capture power for themselves, which enables the personal, family, clan and friends accumulation of wealth. It is as crass as that, for power is always reducible to its personal context. They simply wanted to be white colonizers in non-white bodies heavily afflicted with hallucinatory whiteness, sociopaths all of them.

Fanon further articulates all that distinguishes the Algerian that is the product of the Revolution from that constituted by colonial domination is as follows:

"Whereas the colonized has only a choice between the retraction of his being and a frenzied attempt at reconciliation with the colonizer, the Algerian has brought into existence a new, positive, efficient personality, whose richness is provided less by the trial of strength that he engages in than by his certainty that he embodies a decisive moment of the national consciousness." "Most of the time he has to face problems of building, of organizing, of inventing, the new society that must come into being. That is why colonialism has lost, has irreversibly lost the battle in Algeria." "The Algerian builds, organizes, legislates, plans. Whence his assurance, his firm and resolute language, the energetic cohesion of his positions." (Fanon 1967 pg. 103). The Algerian masses have liberated themselves from the ravages and impediments of the colonial psycho-existential complex through revolutionary struggle against the colonizer. This epic battle is being waged by a unique liberated Algerian, rooted in a national consciousness and wielding power at the micro levels of the matrices of power in a social order in transition liberated, but not yet free of the burden of the colonizer. At this moment in time during the course of the Revolution, this new Algerian wielding power, wasn't she/he not able to transcend time and space thereby muting the attempt of the revolutionary elite to abrogate the power of the masses unto themselves? Fanon's absolute, Revolution, was the entity capable of transcending time and space, as it was the product of the consciousness and action of this new Algerian, thereby ensuring that the agenda of the revolutionary elite could not have succeeded in the course of the Revolution and in the post-Revolutionary period of Algerian history. Why and how then did the revolutionary elite defang the masses and hijack the Revolution in the post-revolutionary period of Algerian history? The answer lies in Fanon's use of the flawed white concept of the Revolution as absolute, for the masses never had the power to wield they reputedly had, for power was always top/down rather than bottom/top between the vanguard and the masses. Compared to the colonial condition, the Revolutionary condition was indeed an advance, but with the departure of the colonizer and the end of the war of liberation, the powerlessness of the masses and the hegemony of the elite were readily apparent. Wide swaths of the masses were subservient to the elite at the level of the idea, which formed the basis of the hegemony of the elite cum the hegemonic oligarchy.

Fanon's embrace of the white concept of Revolution as absolute results in his description of the embrace of the Algerian masses of this absolute as the potent example of Revolution as the only effective means towards liberation from colonial domination. The Algerian Revolution is then Fanon's prime example of the liberationary instrument of Revolution prescribed for the colonized. Fanon states: "Many colonized people have demanded the end of colonization, but rarely like the Algerian people. This refusal of progressive solutions, this contempt for the 'stages' that break the revolutionary torrent and cause the people to unlearn the unshakable will to take everything into their hands at once in order that everything may change, constitutes the fundamental characteristic of the struggle of the Algerian people. And the *moudjahid* which sets forth this position, defends it and makes it triumph, introduces a new element into the classic dialogue of the dominated and the oppressor. The liberation of the individual does not follow national liberation. An authentic national liberation exists only to the precise degree to which the individual has irreversibly begun his own liberation. It is not possible to take one's distance with respect to colonialism without at the same time taking it with respect to the idea that the colonized holds of himself through the filter of colonialist culture." (Fanon 1967 pg. 103). Fanon insists that the commitment of the Algerian masses to the Revolution is total, where the masses constitute a whole engaged in the sole act of excising colonial domination from their land, whatever the cost in lives and in the shortest possible time frame possible. The masses then are engaged in a Jihad and their strategy illustrates their commitment to the Jihad to excise the kaffirun from Algeria. Fanon sees Revolution as absolute and the total commitment of the masses to it, thereby a whole assaulting colonial domination. The masses see and act upon a different worldview, constituted by Islamic discourse, reflected again in Fanon's use of the concept moudjahid to describe the fighters of the Revolution, a concept that describes Muslims engaged in Jihad. Why then does Fanon and the FLN utilise this concept which has no place in their white, secular concept of Revolution as absolute, which is anathema to Islamic discourse as there is only One Absolute? Fanon states that individual liberation does not follow national liberation for national liberation is not attainable without individual liberation preceding it. Fanon insists that you cannot walk away from colonialism without first having walked away from the image of yourself you have embraced, constituted by the colonial psycho-existential complex. In Algeria the war against the colonizer was won but no genuine, authentic national liberation followed because the revolutionary elite and its supplicants amongst the masses did not, failed to first begin and complete the process of individual liberation. Hence their adoration of and lust for white culture and its adoration of wealth and power at the expense of the masses. The Algerian Revolution then proves that you can expel white colonial domination through a successful war against it and then willingly embrace the neo-colonial condition as supplicants and servile non-white indentureds, in spite of your vaunted Revolution. Fanon states: "Such a revolution on the scale of national consciousness and individual consciousness needed to be analyzed." (Fanon 1967 pg. 103). Fanon insists that the Algerian Revolution is the epitome of the anti-colonial Revolution as it was driven by and rooted in the development of individual anti-colonial consciousness which enabled the growth and development of an anti-colonial national consciousness. Fanon cites his evidence for this in the era in which he was writing, but with victory over the colonizer and the evolution of the social order to the 21st century, the reality Fanon never experienced falsifies his position and his entire concept of revolution as absolute. In the closing paragraphs of the article Fanon states: "It is the colonial peoples who must liberate themselves from colonialist domination. Liberation is the total destruction of the colonial system, from the pre-eminence of the language of the oppressor and 'departmentalization,' to the customs union that in reality maintained the former colonized in the meshes of the culture, of the fashion, and of the images of the colonialist." (Fanon 1967 pg. 105). Fanon's standard, his measuring stick, when applied to Algeria of the 21st century, sadly indicates that Algeria, in spite of its epochal Revolution according to Fanon, is yet to be liberated from white supremacist domination best summed up as the neo-colonial condition of the 21st century.

The Specificity of the Algerian Revolution continued

This article was published in El Moudjahid, No. 51, November 1, 1958, in which Fanon continues his exposition of the specificities, even the singularity of the Algerian Revolution in its contribution to the liberation of man. Fanon states: "In the course of different wars of national liberation that have succeeded one another for these past twenty years it was not rare to note a suggestion of hostility, indeed of hate, in the attitude of the colonialist worker toward the colonized. This can be explained by the fact that the retreat of imperialism and the re-conversion of the underdeveloped structures specific to the colonial state are immediately accompanied by economic crises that the workers in the colonialist country are the first to feel." (Fanon 1967 pgs. 144-145). Fanon gives a mechanistic explanation straight out of Marxian economism, which masks the impact of the discourse of white supremacy on the worldview of the white worker on the colonized non-whites of the colonial world and their struggle for liberation. This hate has nothing to do with the economic disruption caused by national liberation of a colony, as the colony remains tied into the unequal trading relations inherited from colonial domination; but is generated by specific brands of nationalist white supremacy and white workers who immerse themselves in this discourse. The old form of colonial imperialism retreats, easily replaced by a non-colonial imperialism, which is much more potent than that of colonial imperialism. This post-colonial imperialism is not dependent on military conquest, but attaches itself to the desires of the newly freed for all things white and western, for modernity and progress. You are then seduced to embrace whiteness, which envelops your body/mind in a soul of servility much more potent than what the colonizer dreamed of, but was unable to realize. Fanon continues: "At the critical point at which the colonized peoples fling themselves into the struggle and demand their independence a critical period elapses in the course of which, paradoxically, the interest of the 'metropolitan' workers and peasants seems to go counter to that of the colonized peoples." (Fanon 1967 pg. 145). It is only in Marxist-Leninist discourse the expectation exists that the interests of the white workers and peasants of the dominant colonizer nation coincide with those of the colonized, therefore the workers and peasants are natural allies of the national liberation struggles of the colonized. In fact, no such solidarity ever existed as the most ardent voices in support of patriotic nationalist colonization

were those of the white workers and peasants. So, it remains in the 21st century where those said voices are loudest in support of actions to destroy the enemies of the Empire. Fanon continues: "To diversify and legitimize this general attitude of the colonialist we find racism, hatred, contempt on the part of the oppressor, and correlatively stultification, illiteracy, moral asphyxiation, and endemic undernourishment in the oppressed." (Fanon 1967 pg. 145). Fanon unveils his Manichean dynamic of colonial domination, where the discourse of white supremacy through its instrument of power of race hatred legitimizes and diversifies the applicability, approach and impact of the discourse on the constituted white colonizer/oppressor. But this discourse also constitutes a condition of being oppressed, of the colonized where the colonized is immersed in a cauldron of: arrested development (material, intellectual and perceptual), of self-hate and contempt and moral deprivation. The condition of the oppressed then enables colonial domination, whilst being the product of colonial domination thereby forming the Manichean duality, for there is no colonizer without the colonial condition and the colonized. Fanon in his search for an instrument of power to destroy the colonizer and the colonial condition simultaneously formulates his discourse of Revolution with the Algerian Revolution as the living model of this instrument of power. To destroy the colonial condition, there must be the explosion and growth of individual consciousness, which drives national consciousness, which are the products of a decision of the masses to engage in a war of liberation to defeat and expel the colonizer from the territory that belongs to the masses, not to the white colonizer. This Manichean duality is then expressed white/colonizer vs. non-white/colonized/liberation fighter. The choice to resist, to engage in revolutionary violence against the colonizer is then the basis of the destruction of the colonial condition and the growth and development of individual and national consciousness. For Fanon, revolutionary violence against the colonizer is the only means to purge the colonial condition, liberate the colonized non-white human and defeat and expel the white colonizer. Proof of the potency of this instrument of liberation, for Fanon, was the course of the Algerian Revolution from 1954 to 1959 as expressed in his writings on Algeria. The Algerians by adopting and embracing the instrument of anti-colonial war and revolutionary violence in 1954 shattered the colonial condition as it impacted the Algerian individual and unleashed the process of the growth and development of national consciousness, both crucially necessary to victory in the anti-colonial war. The Algerians won that war at great cost proving the efficacy of the instrument utilized, but in the course of time post-revolutionary Algeria raises doubts on the efficacy of the instrument to impact the power relations that developed with victory over the colonizer, primarily the power/ force relations between the masses and the revolutionary elite. Fanon died on December 6, 1961 which meant that he never experienced victory over the colonizer in battle, which he valiantly fought for, nor did he experience the power relations of post-revolutionary Algeria. But the question remains valid, and was posed throughout this work interrogating Fanon's discourse in the search for insights into the ability of the revolutionary elite to literally steal the revolution and defang the masses in post-revolutionary Algeria. The issue then is power/ power relations, their nature and dynamic and they have to be focused on from the anti-colonial war in an attempt to understand what happened with victory. For in Fanon's discourse what happened with victory in Algeria was not supposed to have happened as Fanon was using Revolution as an absolute rooted in dialectical/historical materialism which he adopted from the Leninist discourse of historical/dialectical materialism. A discourse rooted in white supremacy formulated for white reality, totally contemptuous of non-white colonized realities. But Fanon's discourse of anti-colonial Revolution in no way fitted into the discourse of Leninist dialectical/historical materialism, in fact Fanon's discourse was anathema to it. Fanon's discourse was then a transplant, an invasive species rejected by Leninist discourse for they were violently incompatible. For Fanon to hold on to his Revolution as absolute, to which he welded his discourse of colonization and the psycho-existential complex with dialectics as his tool of analyses of power relations, he then maintained a veneer of Leninist language in an attempt to mask the grave contradiction of his mixed, mulatto worldview. Fanon openly rejected the basic premise of historical materialism, of the vaunted white revolutionary class, yet he wrote using dialectics as defined by historical materialism. Fanon was then trapped by the manufactured polarity of ideas of his day, of the Cold War, where white ideas were insisting that they were the only alternatives to non-white peoples seeking freedom from white, colonial domination. The white race locked in a bogus war against each other, with the real war being over who wields hegemony over the non-white world, as Mao Zedong understood well. Non-white persons seeking liberation chose then to express their desire for freedom via one of the two white discourses that dominated the ideational structures of the world, or mixtures of both. Fanon was then chafing under this ideational white supremacy, seeking a means to liberate himself at the level of the idea and well advanced in his personal journey of individual consciousness, until death ended this journey in 1961. It is a grave loss to all non-white peoples that Fanon never lived to experience and write about post-revolutionary Algeria. This task now falls to us, especially those as myself, whose lives were impacted and changed by reading the thoughts of Fanon in our youth and grounding with his ideas.

References

Fanon, Frantz (1965): "A Dying Colonialism" Grove Press USA

Fanon, Frantz (1967): "Toward the African Revolution" Grove Press USA

Also by Daurius Figueira

Discourse of Slavery

Massa's White Supremacist Discourse of West Indian Negro Slavery
Deconstructed Volume 1
Massa's White Supremacist Discourse of West Indian Negro Slavery
Deconstructed Volume 2

Frantz Fanon for the 21st Century

Frantz Fanon for the 21st Century Volume 1 Frantz Fanon's Discourse of
Racism and Culture, the Negro and the Arab Deconstructed
Frantz Fanon for the 21st Century Volume 2 Frantz Fanon's Discourse of
Decolonisation and Violence, the Nature of Power and Power Relations of
Neo-colonial African States,
Frantz Fanon for the 21st Century Volume 3 The Algerian Revolution, Islamic
Discourse, the Colonizer and the Discourse of White Supremacy

Standalone

Belize: Human Smuggling, Transnational Organised Crime, Politicians And
Public Servants
Biopower, Racism, State Racism and The Modern/Post Modern North
Atlantic State: Michel Foucault's Genealogy of the Historico-Political
Discourse of Race War Deconstructed

Derek Walcott's Poetry Deconstructed, Its Political and Sociological Discourse Revealed

Transnational Organized Crime and Drug Trafficking in the Second Decade of the 21st Century in the Dominican Republic, Suriname, Venezuela, French Guiana, Martinique and Guadeloupe

The Islamic State and the Muslims of Trinidad and Tobago in the 21st Century

A Deconstruction of Michel Foucault's 1979 Discourse of Neo-Liberalism for the 21st Century

A Deconstruction of Qu'ranic Discourse for the 21st Century

Watch for more at https://www.daurius.com.

About the Author

Daurius Figueira is a researcher, analyst and author located in the anti-Enlightenment and anti-Science discourse/worldview/paradigm specialising in the study of the illicit drug trade, the illicit small arms trade and human smuggling of the Caribbean, Islamic extremism and racism/white supremacy with an emphasis on power relations. You can access his website to experience and download his research papers published online and view his range of books. His website address is: https://www.daurius.com and his blog on the Caribbean is at: https://drugtrade.wordpress.com/

Read more at https://www.daurius.com.